The Arab Spring
Five Years Later

The Arab Spring Five Years Later

Toward Greater Inclusiveness

Volume 1

Hafez Ghanem

Brookings Institution Press
Washington, D.C.

The Brookings Institution is a private nonprofit organization devoted to research,
education, and publication on important issues of domestic and foreign policy. Its
principal purpose is to bring the highest quality independent research and analysis
to bear on current and emerging policy problems. Interpretations or conclusions in
Brookings publications should be understood to be solely those of the authors.

Library of Congress Cataloging-in-Publication data
Names: Ghanem, Hafez, author.
Title: The Arab Spring five years later : toward greater inclusiveness /
   Hafez Ghanem.
Description: Washington, D.C. : Brookings Institution Press, [2016–] |
   Includes bibliographical references and index. | Description based on
   print version record and CIP data provided by publisher; resource not
   viewed.
Identifiers: LCCN 2015045078 (print) | LCCN 2015040104 (ebook) | ISBN
   9780815727194 (epub) | ISBN 9780815727200 (pdf) | ISBN 9780815727187 (pbk.
   : alk. paper)
Subjects: LCSH: Arab Spring, 2010– | Arab countries—History—21st century.
Classification: LCC JQ1850.A91 (print) | LCC JQ1850.A91 G432 2016 (ebook) |
   DDC 909/.097492708312—dc23
LC record available at http://lccn.loc.gov/2015045078

9 8 7 6 5 4 3 2 1

Typeset in Sabon and Myriad Pro

Composition by Cynthia Stock
Silver Spring, Maryland

Contents

Acknowledgments

This book represents the culmination of a three-year academic project undertaken by the Japan International Cooperation Agency (JICA) and the Brookings Institution, exploring how to achieve inclusive growth post-Arab spring, with the goal of contributing to development and stability in the region. The project aims to inform Arab policymakers, thought leaders, as well as bilateral and multilateral development partners and donors that are reviewing their programs and projects to reflect new realities in the region.

This work would not have been possible without the support of many people inside and outside of JICA and Brookings. Kemal Derviş and Homi Kharas provided overall support and guidance. I am particularly grateful to Homi Kharas for his comments on the various papers and on volume 1. Participants in various author workshops provided valuable advice, comments, and suggestions. These included Mayyada Abu Jaber, Perrihan Al-Rifai, Uri Dadush, Shanta Devarajan, Mourad Ezzine, Marc Schifbauer, Djavad Salehi-Isfahani, Ehab Abdou, Tamara Wittes, Bernard Funk, Shinichi Yamanaka, Akihiko Koenuma, Daniela Gressani, Inger Andersen, Heidi Crebo-Rediker, and Andrew Baukol.

Kristina Server provided invaluable management support. Aki Nemoto, Misaki Kimura, and Yamillett Fuentes provided excellent administrative and financial management support. The authors are also grateful to Neil O'Reilly, Christina Golubski, Michael Rettig, and the Brookings Press team led by Janet Walker for their help with editing.

This work was carried out while Hafez Ghanem was a senior fellow at the Brookings Institution, before rejoining the World Bank in March 2015. Hence, it does not necessarily reflect the views of the World Bank.

Brookings is grateful to JICA for its financial and intellectual support of this project. Brookings recognizes that the value it provides is in its absolute commitment to quality, independence, and impact. Activities supported by its donors reflect this commitment, and the analysis and recommendations contained in this volume are not determined or influenced by any donation. The chapters reflect the views of the authors and not the official position of any specific organization.

The Arab Spring
Five Years Later

1

Introduction

This book has a simple message: It is high time for Arab governments and their international partners to focus on the economy and on building inclusive institutions. An almost exclusive focus on divisive political and identity questions since the Arab Spring started in 2010 has contributed to the current malaise. Peace, stability, and democracy in the Arab world will be achieved only if all Arab citizens, especially youth, are fully included in their countries' economy and society and if they feel that their voices are heard in the various institutions of governance. A submessage of this book is that economic growth on its own is not enough. It must be accompanied by social justice.

"The people want to bring down the regime" was the slogan adopted by the young men and women who led the Arab Spring uprisings. The world held its breath as millions of Tunisians and Egyptians poured into Bourguiba Avenue in downtown Tunis and into Tahrir Square in Cairo, demanding an end to autocratic rule and the installation of democratic governance. And the regimes were brought down. Those were exciting days. The democracy fever spread to Bahrain, Yemen, Jordan, and Morocco; massive crowds of demonstrators took to the streets demanding bread, freedom, social justice, and human dignity. Western powers provided military support to an uprising in Libya that deposed a dictator who had come to power through a coup in 1969. And Syrians rose to rid themselves of an autocratic dynasty that had ruled them since 1971. Optimism was the order of the day. Arabs were finally waking up and joining the growing ranks of middle-income countries—like those of Eastern Europe, Latin America, and Asia—who have transited from autocracy to democracy.

But can a country with no democratic tradition and with weak institutions become a well-functioning democracy and improve the lives of its citizens over night? The answer is obviously no. Democratic transitions take years, even decades, to succeed, and there are many twists and turns along the way. Moreover, they can be costly and require heavy human and economic sacrifices. Ask any Arab today if he or she feels that the region is better off than before the Arab Spring. What do you think the answer will be?

Nevertheless, the Arab Spring has brought about a significant, and probably irreversible, change in Arab societies and body politic. I recently asked a Cairo taxi driver what he thought of President el-Sissi. He was full of praise for the newly elected president. However, he was quick to add, "you know we have overthrown two presidents before him (referring to Mohamed Morsi and Hosni Mubarak); so if this one does not deliver we can overthrow him, too." Holding leaders accountable is important for economic, political, and social development. The Arab world appears to be moving toward more open and inclusive governance. But how long will it take for this new spirit to provide results in terms of peace, stability, control of corruption, and economic well-being?

While excessive pessimism should be avoided, it is clear that the Arab transition has taken on a violent, and even scary, character. Thousands have been killed, millions of homes have been destroyed, and more than 15 million Arabs have become either refugees or internally displaced people. Relative to its size, the Arab region has the largest number of failed and fragile states. One fact tells it all. There are thousands of Yemeni refugees in Somalia (an African failed state) today. How long will the chaos in the Arab world last? What can be done to end violent extremism? Can Christians, Jews, Sunnis, Shias, and the myriad of other religions and sects that exist in the Middle East ever live peacefully together? Will anyone be able to stop the organization of the Islamic state, or Daesh, as it is known in Arabic? Will Iraq continue to exist as a nation state? Is the violence in Syria going to end in our lifetime? Will Lebanon ever go back to some semblance of normalcy, with a functioning parliament that meets regularly and is able to pass legislation—and even to elect a president? Are the Arab absolute monarchies sustainable? Will Egypt and Tunisia remain relatively stable? Should Yemen and Libya be written off as unsalvageable failed states? Can the Arab-Israeli conflict be resolved? The answers to those questions are important for the world. Turmoil in the Arab region has global spill-over effects. Thousands of would-be illegal migrants perish every year as they try to cross the Mediterranean to get into Europe. Data on illegal immigration are difficult to obtain, but it seems reasonable to assume that not everybody dies or gets caught and that many thousands succeed in illegally entering Europe. Arabs are the first victims of violent extremism, but they are not the only victims. People in Europe, the United States, and even Japan have suffered from terrorism at the hands of Middle Eastern extremist groups.

This book is not about terrorism or violent extremism. Moreover, it is not about politics nor about democratic transitions. It is about economics. However, I do believe that achieving inclusive economic growth would contribute to peace, stability, and an end to violence in the Arab world. People who feel that their societies provide equal opportunities to all and that their voices are heard in policy discussions, who have good jobs, benefit from quality public services, and have hope for a better future for themselves and their children usually think twice before risking their and their families' standard of living by joining violent or extremist organizations.

Economic growth and social justice are not silver bullets that will, on their own, lead to peace, stability, and democracy in the Arab world. But economic programs that contribute to greater inclusion and higher standards of living should be part of any policy package that aims at peace and stability. The current focus on security measures and political arrangements is not sufficient and should be complemented by economic and social reforms. Successful political transitions in the Arab world will need to be underpinned by transitions to more inclusive economic and social orders.

Inclusive, or shared, growth is defined as growth that leads to higher income and better living standards for all the population and not just the richest group. Empirically, the degree of inclusiveness is often measured by seeing whether the income of the bottom 40 percent of the population has increased and, if so, by how much. Inclusive growth also implies an expansion of the middle class and an improvement in its living standards. Hence an alternative way of measuring inclusiveness is to measure changes in the size of the middle class.

The Arab Spring countries grew at respectable rates of around 4–5 percent a year during the decade preceding the uprisings. Yet all polls showed increasing dissatisfaction with economic conditions during this relatively high growth period. This dissatisfaction could be explained by the fact that growth was not inclusive, and therefore most people's lives were not touched by it. Moreover, people felt that inequality increased, as a small minority, usually well connected to the political elite, received most of the benefits from growth. The sense of unfairness may explain why youth insisted so strongly on the importance of social justice during the Arab Spring uprisings.

Youth, smallholder farmers, and women suffer most from economic and social exclusion in the Arab world. Young people face huge problems finding decent jobs or housing to enable them to get married. They feel that they are excluded from the various decisionmaking processes and are not allowed to provide any input into the decisions that affect their well-being. Poverty in the Arab world is mostly a rural phenomenon, and smallholder farmers are the bulk of the rural poor. Most of the lagging regions in the Arab world, for example, Upper Egypt and Western Tunisia, are populated by smallholder farmers who live under very difficult conditions. Women are an important excluded group. Female labor force participation rates in the Arab region are the lowest in the entire world. Arab women have limited access to productive assets and to credit. Women farmers are a particularly vulnerable group.

In this book I suggest that to achieve inclusive growth, and particularly to deal with the grievances of the three most excluded groups, Arab countries need to focus on four priorities: institutional reforms to improve implementation of policies and programs; reforms of the business environment, with a special emphasis on developing small and medium-size enterprises (SMEs); rural development and support to lagging regions; and improving the quality of education.

Weak institutions and inadequate governance arrangements in Arab countries lead to the adoption of plans and policies that, while they may be technically sound, do not necessarily reflect the needs of different stakeholders. Those institutional and governance weaknesses imply that the plans, programs, and projects are often not implemented. Lack of implementation leads to lower investment and growth. There is a need to render economic institutions in the Arab world more inclusive and responsive to citizens' needs. Arab countries could benefit from the example of successful East Asian economies that put in place consultative processes (including different government departments, the private sector, and civil society) to agree on national development plans and monitor their execution. Effective implementation needs accountability. Each executing agency in charge of a particular sector or policy issue should be held accountable for implementation. There also needs to be a supervisory mechanism that secures the accountability of the institutions and ensures that progress is being made. Institutions usually respond to pressure both from the top (president or prime minister) and from the bottom (citizens).

A focus on expanding small businesses and the SME sector would help grow the middle class and provide greater opportunities for young men and women as business people as well as employees. Real SMEs are rare in the Arab world. Arab economies are dominated by large firms, often operating in sectors that are protected from foreign as well as domestic competition, and by micro enterprises that mostly operate in the informal sector. Those micro enterprises use low technology and therefore provide low wages, and they are predominantly family affairs. They provide livelihoods for millions of Arabs, but they do not offer decent jobs. Developing the Arab SME sector would require reforms to the business environment and competition policies to level the playing field and allow SMEs to grow and compete with large firms, as well as special programs to help SMEs with access to technology, markets, and credit.

Achieving inclusive growth requires paying particular attention to lagging regions that depend mainly on agriculture for livelihood. It is no coincidence that the Arab Spring started in Sidi Bouzid, a poor region in rural Tunisia. Most agricultural producers in the Arab world are smallholder family farmers with plots of less than five hectares. Hence a program for inclusive growth needs to pay special attention to smallholder family farmers. There are six areas where governments could intervene to support smallholder family farmers and help increase their yields: linking smallholders to domestic and international markets to increase their share in value added; adapting financial and investment services to the needs of smallholder family farmers; improving access to land and securing titles; increasing investment in research and extension and adapting them to the needs of smallholders; helping farmers adapt to climate change; and launching special programs for women farmers and youth.

There appears to be a disparity between the skills that Arab youth acquire at schools and universities and those required by employers.

That is why it is also important to consider reforms of education systems. Access to education has improved dramatically in the Arab world over the past two or three decades, but quality has not improved and may even have deteriorated. Students in any of the Arab countries score below the average level on international science and mathematics tests. Low quality of education has an economic cost, as Arab youth are not as productive and competitive as their counterparts around the world. It also has a political cost, as young people who spent many years in the education system are disgruntled because they cannot find jobs that fit with their expectations. Opinion polls indicate that Arab youth are less happy and feel less in control of their lives than youth in other parts of the world. To improve the quality of education, Arab countries need to adjust curricula and teaching methods to reflect the skills and competencies demanded by today's globalized labor market. There is also a need for institutional reforms that hold schools and teachers accountable for student learning.

Peace and stability in the Arab world are global public goods. Therefore, it is in the interest of the international community to help Arab governments achieve inclusive growth that would contribute to peace and stability. The international community needs to remain engaged in the region. However, it may also be necessary to reexamine the nature of this engagement and reorient aid flows toward areas and sectors that directly enhance economic inclusiveness. Examples of such areas would be institution building, support to small-scale enterprises, agriculture and rural development, and education.

2

Spring, but No Flowers

Four years after the start of the Arab revolutions the results are discouraging. Today, most people try to avoid using the term "Arab Spring." Very little has been achieved in the area of democratic reforms. Instead of building vibrant and stable democracies, most of the countries of the Arab Spring revolutions have entered a phase of violence and instability. Political turmoil has been associated with macroeconomic instability, low growth, and high unemployment. The revolutionaries' dreams for more freedom and dignity, and more bread and social justice, appear now even less attainable than before the uprisings.

Of course, country circumstances, and hence outcomes, are different. For a while, before terrorist attacks on the Bardo museum and at Port el Kantaoui near Sousse, Tunisia seemed well on its way to becoming a success story. It achieved significant progress toward democracy after a long and painful transition. Morocco, where the king is leading reform from the top, may be another exception. In general, among the revolting Arab countries, Jordan and Morocco, the two kingdoms, have been more successful in maintaining stability and economic growth than the republics.

Are the discouraging results so far surprising? Probably not. Arab societies are polarized between Islamists and secularists and are also divided along religious, sectarian, and in some countries ethnic grounds. Highly polarized societies typically have a much harder time transitioning to democracy.[1] Arab countries have virtually no experience or culture of democracy. And the institutions necessary for democratic governance—for example, political parties and other civil society

1. Grand (2014) develops the argument on why transitions are more difficult in polarized societies, using examples from third-wave transitions to democracy.

organizations—are either nonexistent or very weak.[2] Under the circumstances, the euphoria and bubbling optimism of 2010–11 appear to have been more the result of wishful thinking than of a serious analysis of the chances for a quick transition to democracy in the Arab world.

But excessive pessimism today may also be a mistake. In 2010–11 Arab populations, especially youth, expressed their desire for more freedom and dignity as well as more bread and social justice. This marked the end of Arab exceptionalism, that is, the view that Arabs were somehow different from other peoples because they placed less value on political freedom and civil liberties.

The Arab Spring is not a season. It is a first and important step on the long road to a new political, social, and economic order. As described by Amin and others (2012), this road will be long and tortuous with several twists and turns, and even setbacks, along the way. Political transitions in the Arab world will take many years and maybe even decades, but they will ultimately succeed as they have in other parts of the world. There is no such thing as Arab exceptionalism.

For this long transition to succeed with minimum human and social costs, political reforms must be accompanied by measures intended to grow the economy and enhance equality and social justice. Economic and political inclusion need to move hand in hand. Sharp divisions over issues of selection of political systems and of national identity are likely to continue in the Arab world, and the current political polarization will not disappear anytime soon. However, consensus could be achieved over issues of economic development and inclusive growth.

Leaders of Arab countries in transition have so far put economic issues on a back burner and focused almost exclusively on highly divisive political questions such as the role of religion in politics. It is time for a change in priorities. Faster and more inclusive economic growth would help achieve political stability and create the social cohesion necessary for building consensus and succeeding in the political transition.

---

2. I stress here the importance of institutions and culture for successful transitions. But other analysts have emphasized different reasons for the difficulty of democratic transformation in the Arab world. Elbadawi and Makdisi (2011) stress the role of oil wealth and of the Arab-Israeli conflict in hindering the development of Arab democracy. Wittes (2008) emphasizes the role of oil rents and geopolitical rivalries in supporting the authoritarian status quo.

The Secularist-Islamist Divide

Arab democratization is particularly difficult because of the high degree of polarization between nationalist-secularists and Islamists. The two groups have very different visions of the type of country and society they want to live in. A Tunisian who believes in secularism and nationalism along the lines advocated by the late president Habib Bourguiba would develop a vision of an independent Tunisian state very close to southern European models. On the other hand, a Tunisian Islamist would dream of living in a Tunisia that is part of a greater caliphate similar to the one built by the early followers of the prophet Mohamed. Constructing a stable and liberal democracy would require that both sides make compromises to reach consensus or that one side succeeds in making the other disappear. Regardless of whether one of the options may be morally superior to the other, it is clear that neither of those options is easy, and certainly neither can be achieved in a short period of time. In view of the deep schism between nationalists and Islamists, Tunisia's achievements over the past four years are remarkable.

Arab nationalist movements started in the late nineteenth century in reaction to European and Ottoman imperialism and continued throughout most of the twentieth century. Nationalism in the Maghreb expressed itself against French, and to a lesser extent Spanish, presence.[3] In Algeria, Amir Abdel Kadir led an armed resistance to the French in the 1830s and 1840s. In Morocco, the revolt of Abdel Karim al-Khattabi led to the eviction of the Spanish army from the Rif Mountains in the early 1920s. Both revolts were ultimately put down by the French military.

The twentieth century, and especially the period following the First World War, witnessed the development of urban-based associations and nationalist political parties seeking independence. Those movements were heavily influenced by ideals of nationalism and socialism brought home by the thousands of Arab soldiers who served in the French army during the war.

The first such party was the Constitution (*destour,* in Arabic) Party in Tunisia, which was created in 1920. Bourguiba, a French-educated

---

3. For a detailed description of the nationalist movements in the Maghreb, see Willis (2014).

lawyer who was the first president of independent Tunisia, rose up the ranks of the Destour but ultimately managed to break up the party and create the Neo-Destour in 1934. The Neo-Destour was much more vocal in its demands for independence and more willing to directly confront the French colonial authorities.

In Morocco, the National Action Bloc was created in the 1930s and transformed itself into the Independence (*istiqlal,* in Arabic) Party in 1944. Like the Neo-Destour, Morocco's Istiqlal was mostly an urban party supported by the new intellectual and business elites.

Modern nationalist sentiment in Egypt dates back to the late nineteenth century, when Ahmed Orabi, at the time head of the Egyptian armed forces, revolted in 1879 against the khedive, who represented the Ottoman Empire.[4] Like Abdel Kadir and Abdel Karim al-Khattabi, Orabi's revolt failed, as the British intervened to support the khedive. Orabi's army was defeated in 1882, he was exiled, and Egypt became a British protectorate.

Orabi's nationalist mantle was taken over by Saad Zaghloul, a civilian, who started a revolution against British colonial rule in 1919. Zaghloul established the Wafd, which continued to be Egypt's largest party, winning 179 parliamentary seats out of 211 in the 1924 elections and 157 seats (with 89 percent of the vote) in 1936, until it was dissolved by Gamal Abdel Nasser in 1952. Throughout its history the Wafd was in constant conflict with the king and with the British, who effectively ruled Egypt despite its nominal independence in 1922.

The situation in Jordan and Yemen was different.[5] Yemen was divided into North and South. The North became independent of Ottoman rule in 1918 and was ruled by hereditary imams until a revolution toppled the system in 1962 (with Egyptian military support). The South was under British rule and then local communist rule in the 1960s. The two parts of Yemen were united in 1990. In addition to the North-South divide, Yemen is also divided along sectarian lines between Sunnis and Shias.

Unlike Egypt, Morocco, Tunisia, and Yemen, which have a relatively long history as separate nation states, Jordan was created in 1922 as

---

4. See Ghanem (2014a) for a more detailed exposition of Egypt's political economy and history.

5. See Owen (2012).

a prize for Amir Abdullah, of the Hashemite family of Arabia, for his support to the allies against the Ottomans during the First World War. Jordan was part of the British mandate that covered Palestine and only became an independent kingdom under Abdullah in 1946. Jordan's kings, especially King Hussein, who ruled from 1953 to 1999, led the nationalist movement with strong support from Bedouin tribes.

As described by Muasher (2014), Arab independence struggles took a distinctly nationalist flavor, and their leaders adopted secular values. Owen (2012) argues that for the first generation of postindependence Arab leaders, establishment and protection of national sovereignty was the most important goal. This necessitated the expansion of the military and the development of a middle-class officer cadre with an intense sense of patriotism. The military ruled directly in Egypt (under Nasser, Anwar Sadat, and Hosni Mubarak) and Yemen (under Ali Abdullah Saleh) and played a key role in protecting the regimes in Tunisia, Jordan, and Morocco, where President Bourguiba, King Hussein, and King Hassan II established themselves as leaders of the nationalist movements in their respective countries.

Arab nationalism did not embrace democracy. Postindependence governments questioned the legitimacy of democratic governance because it was supported by elites who collaborated with colonial powers. On the other hand, the nationalist movement was a force for modernization. It called for the separation of state and religion, greater social justice, women's rights, and support for a cultural and artistic renaissance.

Islamism could be viewed as the antithesis of Arab nationalism. Modern political Islam has its roots in Egypt, where it started in 1928 with the creation of the Muslim Brotherhood by Hassan al-Banna. The Brotherhood continues to exist in Egypt today, although it has been designated a terrorist organization and banned by the administration of President Abdel-Fattah el-Sissi. It has offshoots across the Arab world. It is present in Jordan, where its political arm, the Islamic Action Front, is an important opposition actor. Morocco has two Islamist parties: the moderate Justice and Development Party is currently leading the coalition government, while the hard-line Justice and Charity Party is not a legally recognized party and does not participate in the formal political process. Inspired by the Muslim Brotherhood, Tunisian Islamists founded the Movement of the Islamic Tendency in 1981 and then changed its name to Ennahda, which means *renaissance* in Arabic, in

1989. Ennahda is participating in Tunisia's coalition government. Islah is the Brotherhood's offshoot in Yemen, and it joined the government and the national dialogue after the 2011 revolution.

The Brotherhood was created as a pan-Islamic social and political movement, partly in response to the fall of the Ottoman Empire and the abolition of the caliphate in Turkey by Mustapha Kemal Ataturk. This abolition was seen as an important setback by many pious Muslims, including al-Banna, who considered the caliphate a necessity in Islam. This put the Brotherhood in direct confrontation with Arab nationalists.[6]

The Brotherhood was based on two important principles. The first is the adoption of sharia law as the basis for conducting the affairs of state and society. For the Brotherhood, Islam is a state as well as a religion. This is sometimes understood to imply that secular ideas are inherently un-Islamic and therefore Muslims who call for a secular state could be considered nonbelievers. The Brotherhood holds conservative views on gender equality and the role of women in society. They argue for a "modest" dress for women and the separation of the sexes at schools and workplaces. They also believe that cultural products should reflect the Islamic nature of society, and they have called for censorship of books and movies that they consider un-Islamic. Thus the Brotherhood has often been at odds with Arab cultural and artistic elites.

The second principle is to unify Islamic states and free them from foreign imperialism. Hence the Brotherhood considers any individual Arab country as just one small part of a large Islamic empire (or caliphate) stretching from Spain to Indonesia. A previous general guide (or chairman) of the Brotherhood in Egypt, Mohamed Akef, generated an outcry when he stated in an interview with the magazine *Rosa al Yusuf*, "To hell with Egypt."[7] Of course, he meant to emphasize the pan-Islamic ambitions of his organization, but nationalists interpreted his statement as meaning that the Brotherhood does not care about Egypt.

The Brotherhood has officially announced that it supports democracy and rejects violence. However, its detractors argue that it is difficult to reconcile democratic values that imply that the people have the final say regarding their affairs with an Islamic approach that

6. For a history of the Brotherhood, see Wickham (2013).
7. Shoeb (2006).

believes that God's word as presented in the Quran and the Hadith (the Prophet's sayings) should be the basis of all constitutions and laws. The Brotherhood's stated belief that Islam is a state as well as a religion seems incompatible with democratic governance.

The Brotherhood's doctrine seems to have embraced violence and the concept of jihad, at least in its initial years. According to Hassan al-Banna, jihad was the obligation of every Muslim. In one of his tracts he states that

> today the Muslims, as you know, are compelled to humble themselves before non-Muslims and are ruled by unbelievers. . . . Hence, it has become an individual obligation, which there is no evading, on every Muslim to prepare his equipment, to make up his mind to engage in jihad, and to get ready for it until the opportunity is ripe and God decrees a matter which is sure to be accomplished.[8]

Today's leaders of the Brotherhood insist that they no longer espouse violence. Their nationalist detractors disagree and label them as terrorists. This debate is probably going to continue for a while and will not be resolved any time soon. However, one thing is clear. Al-Banna's words appear to describe current positions of avowedly terrorist organizations like al-Qaeda and the Islamic State

Scholars disagree as to whether the Brotherhood has changed and has embraced democratic values. Wickham (2013) argues that the Brotherhood has evolved, especially owing to some of its members' participation in political life. She believes that this experience has made the Brotherhood more open to political debate and dialogue and more accepting of democratic values. In a sense, the Brotherhood joined the formal political system to change it but ended up being changed by it. Nevertheless, she explains, one cannot conclude that the Brotherhood has embraced the liberal and inclusive ethos of democracy because its insistence on an Islamic frame of reference implies the existence of an authority above the electorate. Bradley (2012) is less nuanced. He argues that the belief that the Brotherhood has evolved has more to do with its recruitment of effective spokesmen who spout the virtues of its prodemocracy platform than with any real change in its position.

---

8. Quoted in Wendell (1978, p. 150).

Regardless of the issues of acceptance of democracy and rejection of violence, the other differences between nationalists and Islamists appear irreconcilable. They include national versus religious identity, personal liberties, women's role in society, and the role of the arts and culture. Arab and Muslim society seems to be divided right down the middle, and the polarization appears to be getting worse every day with the emergence of groups like the Islamic State and the development of jihadist ideologies among migrant populations in Europe and North America.

Different Transition Experiences

This polarization of Arab society greatly complicated the transition process. Nowhere is this more evident than in Egypt. Tunisia faces the same challenges as Egypt but so far has succeeded in maintaining national unity and building a democratic consensus. Yemen's transition is in deep trouble, but it is not only owing to the secularist-Islamist divide. Yemen's troubles are also caused by ethnic and sectarian differences. The two monarchies, Jordan and Morocco, have been more successful in maintaining stability, but the pace of democratic reforms has been slow.

Egypt

Egypt is by far the largest Arab country, and its transition, which has been particularly messy, has attracted world attention. Hence it makes sense to study it in some detail.

The military was put in charge of the transition in Egypt, and Marshal Mohamed Hussein Tantawi, Mubarak's minister of defense, became the de facto head of state after Mubarak's resignation. The first political disagreement he had to deal with was on the question of the timing of elections and the writing of a new constitution. After the dissolution of Mubarak's National Democratic Party, the Brotherhood was the only organized group left in the country and therefore would win in any early election. They pushed for elections to take place before a constitution was written. The liberal, nationalist, Nasserist, and leftist parties wanted time to prepare and organize their bases. Therefore they argued for agreement on a new constitution before elections. At this point the Brotherhood promised not to field candidates for more than 50 percent of the seats in parliament, so that they would rule only in a coalition government, and they also promised not to field a presidential candidate. The military sided with the Brotherhood and started preparing for elections before the constitution.

In spite of a boycott by the revolutionary youth and continued demonstrations and unrest, elections for the lower house of Parliament took place in three stages between November 28, 2011, and January 8, 2012. As expected, the results were catastrophic for the secularists. The Brotherhood won 37.5 percent of the popular vote, which translated into 45 percent of the seats in Parliament. The Salafists came in second, winning 27.8 percent of the popular vote and 25 percent of the seats in Parliament. Thus Egypt's first postrevolution parliament had a crushing Islamist majority of 70 percent. Elections for the upper house were carried out on January 29 and February 22, 2012. They elicited little enthusiasm, and voter turnout was low. Islamists won nearly 80 percent of the seats, with the Brotherhood holding an absolute majority of about 58 percent.

The Brotherhood-dominated parliament elected a constituent assembly to start drafting Egypt's postrevolutionary constitution. It included 66 Islamists out of 100 members. It had only 6 women and 5 Copts. Secular parties boycotted the assembly, and ultimately the courts declared it unconstitutional because members of Parliament elected themselves to the assembly. Agreement was reached between secularists and Islamists on the structure of the second constituent assembly, but the secularists claimed that the Islamists broke that agreement. Many secular parties followed the call of Mohamed el-Baradei (liberal) and Hamdeen Sabbahi (Nasserist) to boycott the second constituent assembly. Other groups, including Coptic Church representatives, also joined the boycott. According to a poll carried out by Al-Ahram news agency, more than 80 percent of Egyptians wanted the constituent assembly to be reformed to better reflect all forces in society. The schism between the Islamists and the rest of society appeared to be getting wider.

In the meantime, a presidential election was held in two rounds, the first round on May 23 and 24, 2012, and the second on June 16 and 17, 2012. The Brotherhood broke its second political promise and fielded a presidential candidate. In fact, it fielded two candidates. Its preferred candidate was Khayrat al-Shatter, a millionaire businessman and deputy general guide of the Brotherhood. However, al-Shatter had legal problems that could disqualify him. That is why the Brotherhood also fielded a second candidate, Mohamed Morsi, president of its political party (Freedom and Justice). This earned Morsi the nickname "the spare-tire candidate." In the end, the Brotherhood was right: al-Shatter was disqualified, and Morsi became the official Brotherhood candidate.

The military stated that it was not supporting any political group or candidate. However, most Egyptians felt that it supported Ahmed Shafik, a former general of the Egyptian air force and the last prime minister under Mubarak. The choice of Shafik as the standard-bearer of the liberal-nationalist-military alliance was unfortunate. He was too closely associated with the Mubarak regime. It would have been difficult for the people of Tahrir Square to vote for him. Another liberal candidate, Amr Moussa (a former minister of foreign affairs and secretary general of the Arab League) presented himself in the elections, but he did not receive much support from the military and its followers.

Morsi won the first-round presidential elections and Shafik came in second (table 2-1). Thus the second round was a runoff between those two. In that first round, Islamists (Morsi and Abul Foutouh) obtained 42.3 percent of the vote. The liberals (Shafik and Moussa) won 34.8 percent, and the Nasserist Sabbahi 20.7 percent. Sabbahi's strong showing demonstrates that the Nasserist and leftist message still attracts substantial support in Egypt, particularly among the working class. It is noteworthy that Sabbahi won pluralities in Egypt's two largest cities, Cairo and Alexandria.

Morsi won the second round of presidential elections with 51.7 percent of the vote to Shafik's 48.3 percent. Many secularists voted for Morsi because they did not want to support someone they considered to be a Mubarak clone. Others simply stayed home on election day. It is hard to predict what the outcome of the elections (and hence of the overall transition) would have been had the liberal-nationalist-military coalition selected someone other than Shafik as their standard-bearer. But an opinion poll by Al-Ahram indicates that had the second round of presidential elections been between Mohamed Morsi and Amr Moussa, Moussa would have won with 77.6 percent of the vote to only 22.4 percent for Morsi.

Egyptians of all political leanings, who were worried that the elections might get rigged in favor of Shafik, celebrated Morsi's electoral victory. His inauguration on June 30, 2012, was reminiscent of the day that

TABLE 2-1. Results of First-Round Presidential Elections, Egypt, 2012

Candidate	Political current	Share of vote (percent)
Mohamed Morsi	Muslim Brotherhood	24.8
Ahmed Shafik	Liberal	23.7
Hamdeen Sabbahi	Nasserist	20.7
Abdel Moneim Abul Fotouh	Moderate Islamist	17.5
Amr Moussa	Liberal	11.1
Others		2.2

Source: Egyptian Supreme Committee for Elections.

Mubarak resigned. Tahrir Square was filled with huge crowds representing all political forces. A few weeks later Morsi fired Field Marshal Tantawi from his post as minister of defense and replaced him with General el-Sissi. He also appointed a new chief of staff of the armed forces. This move was widely supported. Democracy seemed to be working, as the elected civilian president was taking control of the military.

Morsi promised to be the president of all Egyptians and to appoint two vice presidents, a woman and a Copt. But those promises were not kept, and the euphoria following Morsi's election quickly dissipated as Egyptians slowly came to believe that he was only the Brotherhood's president.

The Brotherhood's worst mistake occurred on November 22, when Morsi issued a seven-article constitutional declaration. Article 2 stated that all decrees, constitutional declarations, or laws issued by President Morsi since his inauguration on June 30 could not be appealed or canceled by any authority of the country (effectively ending parliamentary and judicial oversight) and that all pending lawsuits against his decisions were void. Article 6 authorized the president to take any measure he saw fit to protect the revolution and safeguard national unity (effectively giving him unlimited dictatorial powers). Reaction against this declaration was quick and vehement. The president was forced to retract and annul his ill-fated declaration, but the damage to his stature and to the Brotherhood's democratic image was already done.

The Brotherhood decided to quickly push through a new constitution before the judiciary could dissolve the second Islamist-dominated constituent assembly, which was being boycotted by nearly all secular groups. The new constitution was passed by referendum that was carried out in two stages on December 15 and 22, 2012. It was approved by a 63.8 percent majority, but voter turnout was only 32.9 percent, and a majority of voters in Cairo (the capital and largest city) voted against the constitution. The new constitution reflected an Islamist vision of Egypt rather than a broad societal consensus. Copts were against this constitution because it did not sufficiently protect minority rights. Women's groups opposed it because it did not ensure equality of the sexes, and the media opposed it because it did not protect freedom of the press.

An open confrontation emerged between the Brotherhood and nearly all sections of Egypt's elite: the judiciary, the media, artists, intellectuals, and of course the deep state (key civil servants and security personnel). Large segments of Egyptian society felt that President Morsi and his supporters were imposing their vision of postrevolution Egypt without sufficient consultation. For many among them it became an existential struggle. Two political parties that historically have been sworn adversaries, Sabbahi's Nasserists and el-Sayyid al-Badawi's New Wafd, agreed to coordinate and join el-Baradei's Salvation Front against the Brotherhood. Even Abul Foutouh's moderate Islamists joined forces with the secular parties in the Salvation Front.

By early 2013 Morsi's position was starting to look shaky. He was facing a united opposition of secularists and moderate Islamists who were supported by the revolutionary youth, the judiciary, the media, and the cultural elite. Those running large businesses also joined the ranks of Morsi's opponents because the economy was quickly heading toward a major crisis. Officially, the military, the police, and the civil service were neutral. However, it was an open secret that those intensely nationalist institutions, filled by Mubarak appointees, did not trust the Brotherhood.

Thus when a group of revolutionary youth started the Tamarod (rebellion, in Arabic) movement and began collecting signatures on a petition for early presidential elections, they received tremendous moral support from political, cultural, and media elites as well as financial support from the business community. They claimed to have collected 22 million signatures on the petition, far more than the 13 million votes that Mr. Morsi obtained on the second round of elections. They then organized massive anti-Morsi demonstrations in all Egyptian cities. At this point the military stepped in with an ultimatum to both sides in the confrontation (but clearly mainly directed at Morsi) to reach a compromise. Otherwise, they said, they would impose their own road map for a new transition.

Morsi rejected opposition demands for early elections as well as the military's ultimatum to reach a compromise that would be acceptable to the Egyptian street. He insisted that he was the legitimate president of Egypt and would complete his four-year term in office. With the benefit of hindsight it would have made much more sense for Morsi to negotiate a compromise with the opposition and with the military. It was clear that Egypt's transition was in trouble and a change of direction was needed. It may still have been possible for him to lead this change and start a process of healing and national reconciliation. But he chose not to, and on July 3, he was deposed. At least as many people swarmed into Tahrir Square to celebrate his fall as had celebrated his election a year earlier.

The military was once more made responsible for managing Egypt's transition. It quickly appointed the head of the constitutional court, Adly Mansour, as interim president, and he appointed a government of technocrats headed by a well-known economist, Hazem al-Biblawi, as prime minister. The military also announced a road map for a return to normal governance that included a referendum on a new constitution and presidential and parliamentary elections.

The first step on the road map was concluded when a new constitution, prepared by a committee chaired by Amr Moussa, was approved by referendum on January 14 and 15, 2014. The participation rate of nearly 39 percent and the 98 percent yes vote were higher than those obtained by the Muslim Brotherhood–backed 2012 constitution.

Transparency International's team that observed the referendum stated that "the political context in the run-up to the referendum impaired conditions to hold a fair and free referendum when compared with international standards."[9] The assessment pointed out that the interim authorities took some steps that limited freedom of expression, association, and assembly and that civil society's capacity to represent the voice of the people had thereby been greatly reduced. According to Transparency International, government officials as well as public and private media outlets campaigned vigorously for a yes vote and did not

---

9. Transparency International Observation Mission Egypt Constitutional Referendum, preliminary report, January 16, 2014, p. 2.

provide an opportunity for the opposition to express its views. Moreover, activists who called for a no vote or for boycotting the referendum faced repression.

In spite of those problems, nearly all foreign observers agreed that the referendum reflected the will of the Egyptian people. How could one explain Egyptians' supporting two very different constitutions in a space of a few months? The answer probably is that it was not the same Egyptians who went to vote each time. Participants in the Brotherhood-organized referendum were mostly young and male, while those who participated in the second referendum were mostly female and middle aged. According to this view, the schism between secularists and Islamists in Egypt has a gender as well as a generational dimension. It also seems to have a rural-urban dimension, with the Brotherhood usually garnering more support in rural areas.

The second step of the road map was completed in May 2014, when Field Marshall el-Sissi was easily elected president in a contest in which his only adversary was Sabbahi, leader of the Nasserist Party. Thus Egypt chose a popular officer as its new president, and people started immediately to compare him with Gamal Abdel Nasser, who led the revolt against the king in 1952 and who suppressed the Muslim Brotherhood in the 1950s and 1960s.

The third and last remaining step of the road map is the parliamentary election, which is now expected to take place by late 2015. According to the new electoral law, only 20 percent of the 540 elected seats in parliament will be assigned to party lists, while 80 percent will be assigned to individuals running in their constituencies. It is expected that this arrangement will hinder the development of a strong and unified opposition block in Parliament

The struggle between nationalists and Islamists continues, even as the road map is being implemented. The Brotherhood was designated a terrorist organization, its assets were confiscated, and its leaders, including Morsi, were put in jail. Brotherhood activists and demonstrators face severe repression as they could be prosecuted as members of a terrorist organization. Demonstrations and street violence have become a common occurrence, and many deaths have been reported.

Islamists are fighting back, often using violence and terrorism, but the Brotherhood itself denies involvement in those acts. The security situation remains volatile, as Islamist groups carry out armed attacks against police and military targets as well as against some civilian targets. Perhaps the new regime's greatest challenge is in northern Sinai, where the group Ansar Beit al-Maqdis, which has sworn allegiance to the Islamic State of Iraq and Syria, is active and is targeting security personnel and economic installations.

As could be expected, the cycle of violence and counterviolence had a negative impact on human rights. Amnesty International states on its website that

> [in] the years following the "January 25 revolution" the human rights outlook in Egypt remains grim. . . . Egypt has suffered a number of human rights setbacks, not least since the removal of Mohamed Morsi from the presidency in July 2013, including the killing of up to 1,000 people on August 14, 2013, during the dispersal of sit-ins by his supporters by the security forces. . . . Some of the names strongly associated with the "January 25 revolution," including one of the founders of April 6 Youth Movement, Ahmed Maher, and blogger and opposition activist Alaa Abdel Fattah, find themselves behind bars for breaking the repressive new assembly law.[10]

What will happen next in Egypt? There are at least two possible scenarios. The more pessimistic scenario would be that the violence will continue so that the el-Sissi administration will find that it needs to maintain repressive measures that curtail political and civil liberties. Hence under this scenario Egypt's democratic transition fails and the country remains more or less where it was before the Arab Spring. The second and more optimistic scenario likens Field Marshall el-Sissi to General de Gaulle of France. Under this scenario el-Sissi succeeds in stabilizing the security situation and then proceeds to implement democratic reforms. Thus Egypt could gradually evolve into a full-fledged democracy. At this point it is not clear which scenario is more likely. Supporters of el-Sissi believe that he will lead the country toward full-fledged democracy, while his detractors, especially from

10. See Amnesty International website www.amnestyusa.org/our-work/countries/middle-east-and-north-africa/egypt).

the Brotherhood, argue that Egypt is turning into a military dictatorship even more repressive than the one under Mubarak.

Tunisia

Tunisia's transition has been very different from Egypt's, and much less messy. The first difference concerns the role of the military. The Tunisian army avoided confrontation with demonstrators yet played a pivotal role ensuring security and minimizing violence. Most important, it did not intervene directly in the political process and created enough space for the civilian politicians to manage the transition.

Thus whereas in Egypt the minister of defense became the de facto head of state after Mubarak's resignation, in Tunisia the president of Parliament played that role, but the real power remained with the prime minister. Initially Mohamed Ghannouchi, who was prime minister under Zine al-Abidine Ben Ali, remained at this post, but faced with increasing protest he had to step down a month after Ben Ali's departure.

The second major difference between the Egyptian and Tunisian experiences is that Tunisia decided to agree on a constitution before electing a permanent government and head of state. On February 27, 2011, Beji Caid Essebsi, who had held several ministerial positions under President Bourguiba, was selected as transitional prime minister to replace Ghannouchi. He formed a government of independent ministers on March 7, with the clear objective of electing a constituent assembly. He declared that no member of his government would be allowed to run in the forthcoming constituent assembly elections.

Essebsi succeeded in his mission. Elections were held in October 2011 and were considered a model for the rest of the Arab world. They were held peacefully, and the participation rate was high, as 51 percent of eligible voters actually cast their ballots. Foreign and domestic election monitors praised the process for its transparency and fairness.

A third important difference with the Egyptian experience is that the Tunisian electoral system of a one-round proportional representation made it difficult for any single party to obtain an outright majority. Thus the Islamists in Tunisia did not control a majority of the seats of the assembly, as they had in Egypt, even though they got most votes. The Ennahda Party obtained 89 seats out of the assembly's 217 and had to form a coalition with two secular parties, the Congrés pour la République, which won 29 seats, and Ettakatol, which won 20 seats.

Thus it was agreed that Ennahda's Hamadi Jebali take over as prime minister, while the Congrés's Moncef Marzouki become president and head of state and Ettakatol's Mustapha Ben Jaffar become speaker of the constituent assembly.

As in Egypt, the period 2011–15 was marred by protests, violence, and several political assassinations. Tunisia had to carry out its own war on terror at a time when the economy was either stagnant or declining and social tensions were mounting. Moreover, instability in neighboring Libya and the increase in Libyans' seeking refuge in Tunisia and the transfer of weapons through porous borders rendered the situation even more challenging.

Tunisia faced the same disagreements over the constitution as Egypt had. Islamists wanted sharia to be the basis for all laws, and they favored a parliamentary form of government. However, unlike Egypt, Tunisia has a vibrant and powerful civil society, particularly labor unions. Union interventions succeeded in pushing Islamists as well as secularists to make concessions and reach a consensus on the constitution. Ennahda also proved itself much more flexible and open to compromise than the Muslim Brotherhood in Egypt.[11] In addition to reaching consensus on a constitution, Tunisians also agreed to select a neutral government of technocrats to manage the constitutional referendum and the ensuing parliamentary and presidential elections.

Parliamentary elections were held in October 2014, and a secular party, Nida Tounes, led by Beji Caid Essebsi, won most seats in Parliament but not an outright majority. In December Essebsi won the presidential elections. He appointed a respected politician, Habib Essid, as prime minister, and Essid formed a broad coalition government that included Ennahda, who came in second in the parliamentary elections. Thus Tunisia will continue to be governed by consensus between its strong secular and Islamist forces. Maintaining this coalition will certainly be difficult, but the country appears to be well on its way to becoming a full-fledged democracy, the first in the Arab world. However, Tunisia's transition is being threatened by terrorism. Attacks on tourists at the Bardo museum in Tunis and on a beach in Sousse

11. It is sometimes argued that the fall of the Brotherhood government in Egypt was at least one of the factors that prompted Ennahda to make serious concessions to secular parties.

have had a devastating effect on Tunisia's important tourism sector and hence its overall economy. These attacks underline the fragility of Tunisia's transition to democracy.

Yemen

The problems facing Yemen's transition are more related to sectarian and regional differences, as well as interference by al-Qaeda in the Arabian Peninsula (AQAP), than to the secular-Islamist divide. Hence they are even more complicated than the problems faced by the Egyptians and Tunisians. The transition in Yemen has gotten so out of hand that it is not only the future of democracy in the country that is threatened but also Yemen's continued existence as a unified state.

The Arab Spring spread from Tunisia to Egypt and then to Yemen, where President Ali Abdullah Saleh had been in power for almost thirty-four years. Saleh initially refused to step down and resisted for many months until November of 2011, when he finally signed an agreement brokered by the neighboring countries of the Gulf Cooperation Council under which he agreed to hand over power to his vice president, Abdel-Rabbuh Mansour Hadi, in return for amnesty for himself and his inner circle. During the long months before the agreement there were sustained demonstrations and unrest and the country was pushed to the brink of civil war.

The protracted political battle in Sana'a (Yemen's capital city), and the inevitable power vacuum during those long months, led to power grabs by different factions and tribal groups. The extreme north of the country fell under the control of the Houthis, a Zaydi rebel group, and the southern secessionist movement (Hirak) gained more ground.[12] Armed groups and tribal forces controlled different parts of Sana'a. Perhaps most dangerous, the power vacuum and general chaos allowed AQAP to expand its operations in Yemen and to use Yemen as a base for attacking other countries.

Hadi was elected president on February 21, 2012 (his was the only name on the ballot), to lead a two-year transition that was to include agreement on a new constitution and the organization of free elections. Former president Saleh remained in Sana'a and continued to represent an important political force, which tended to complicate things

---

12. Zaydis are a sect that emerged in the eight century out of Shia Islam.

for his successor. A new coalition government was formed headed by Mohamed Salim Basindwa, a prominent opposition figure and a former minister of foreign affairs who resigned from the ruling party in the early 2000s. Cabinet posts were evenly divided between the opposition Joint Meeting Parties (which includes Islah) and Saleh's General People's Congress. The government started to organize a national dialogue in which all stakeholders participated to prepare a new constitution.

The National Dialogue conference proved inclusive and tackled all the important issues, but it was not able to complete its work by September 18, 2013, as initially planned. The status of the South in a new Yemen was a key stumbling block. Southern representatives, supported by the northern Houthis, argued for a federal structure in which the South and the North would have equal status. But the General People's Congress opposed the idea. Saleh, who remained head of the party, even called it treason.

In the meantime the security situation continued to deteriorate. There was an attempt to assassinate the prime minister as well as an attack on the ministry of defense in which fifty-six people were killed and hundreds were injured. Al-Qaeda in the Arabian Peninsula continued its operations in Yemen, and in a widely publicized event the United States closed all of its embassies in the region because of a threat that reportedly emanated from Yemen.

Protests erupted in Sana'a in the summer of 2014 after the government removed fuel subsidies. Those protests and the violent police reaction to them provided a reason for Houthi forces to march into Sana'a in September 2014. The Houthi capture of Sana'a faced so little resistance that some observers argued that Saleh was implicitly supporting them to take revenge on the Islah Party, a Sunni Islamist group that is naturally opposed to the Zaydi Houthis. The Houthis were also seen as a threat to AQAP, another Sunni organization.

Naturally, Hadi was greatly weakened by the Houthi capture of the capital city. Moreover, he was expelled from the General People's Congress because he supported United Nations sanctions against Saleh that bar him from political office. This meant that in addition to losing control of Sana'a, he lost his political base. The UN brokered an agreement between the victorious Houthis and the other political factions. A new prime minister, Khaled Bahah, a former ambassador to the UN,

was named to lead a broad coalition government in which both the
Houthis and Hirak were represented. However, with a weakened president Hadi, it was inevitable that this arrangement would be short lived.

On February 8, 2015, the Houthis announced the takeover of the
Yemeni government, dissolving Parliament and replacing it with a
551-member National Transitional Council, which will elect a five-
person presidential council. In the interim it was decided that an
eighteen-member security commission will act as Yemen's executive
branch. The Houthis also replaced the heads of offices of the president
and the prime minister.

At present, Hadi and his government are in exile in Saudi Arabia.
The Saudis are leading a coalition that is bombarding the Houthis in
Yemen. This is clearly not the end of the story in Yemen.

Jordan

Like Egypt, Tunisia, and Yemen, Jordan was rocked in January 2011
by street demonstrations and widespread protest. But unlike in the
three republics, the people called not for a regime change but rather
for a reform of the existing regime. Jordan's king Abdullah II is a
descendant of the prophet Mohamed and is seen as a legitimate ruler.
In addition, he garners huge support from the tribal areas and from
the military. Muasher (2014) argues that because the Muslim Brotherhood has always been allowed to operate legally in Jordan as a
charitable organization, it adopted moderate policies and saw itself
as part of the regime. On the other hand, Jordan has a large population of Palestinian origin, and tensions between it and the Jordanians could create some instability. More recently a huge influx of
Syrian refugees further complicated the country's economic, social,
and political situation.

The king reacted to the protest movement by deciding to lead a process of reform from above. He set up a royal committee to consider
constitutional changes. However, the committee was dominated by
conservatives and came up with little in terms of recommendations.
Perhaps the greatest achievement from this exercise was the creation,
for the first time in Jordan, of a constitutional court. The king also
decided to limit the scope of the state security courts, dominated by
military judges, which earned him rare praise from the opposition.

Most observers agree that the reforms carried out so far have been very limited, and that there is a risk of more protests and instability.[13] Because of his legitimacy and popularity, King Abdullah II is in a position to implement gradual reforms so as to steer his country toward full democracy while avoiding the huge human and economic costs caused by turmoil and instability experienced in Egypt, Tunisia, and Yemen.

Morocco

Like King Abdullah II, King Mohammed VI of Morocco is a descendant of the prophet Mohamed, is popular, and is seen as legitimate by the majority of the population. Faced with a similar wave of protests in 2011, King Mohammed VI went further than his Jordanian counterpart in implementing political reforms. As in Jordan, a committee was created to amend the constitution. But the amendments proposed by the Moroccan committee went much further than those proposed and implemented in Jordan.

The new constitution was adopted by referendum in July 2011. It strengthened the powers of the prime minister and of Parliament, as well as the independence of the judiciary. It enshrined more political and social rights and called for a more open and decentralized governance system, laying the groundwork for more-inclusive economic growth. As prescribed by the new constitution, the king appointed the leader of the party that won most seats in Parliament (Abdelilah Benkiraine, leader of the moderately Islamist Justice and Development Party [PJD]) as prime minister.

The new Moroccan constitution went further than the Jordanian one, but it did not significantly reduce the powers of the king, who continues to be the dominant political figure in Morocco. King Mohammed VI will continue to lead the transition. Evolutionary change carries the risk of a slowdown, or even a halt, in the reform process as powerful interest groups feel threatened and attempt to block the transition. This could lead to disappointment and frustration among the population, especially the youth, and hence to political unrest. That is why King Mohammed VI will need to remain one step ahead of the Moroccan street, implementing reforms at a pace that is fast enough to maintain

13. For example, Muasher (2014).

FIGURE 2-1. Freedom Index, Arab Countries in Transition, 2010 and 2015

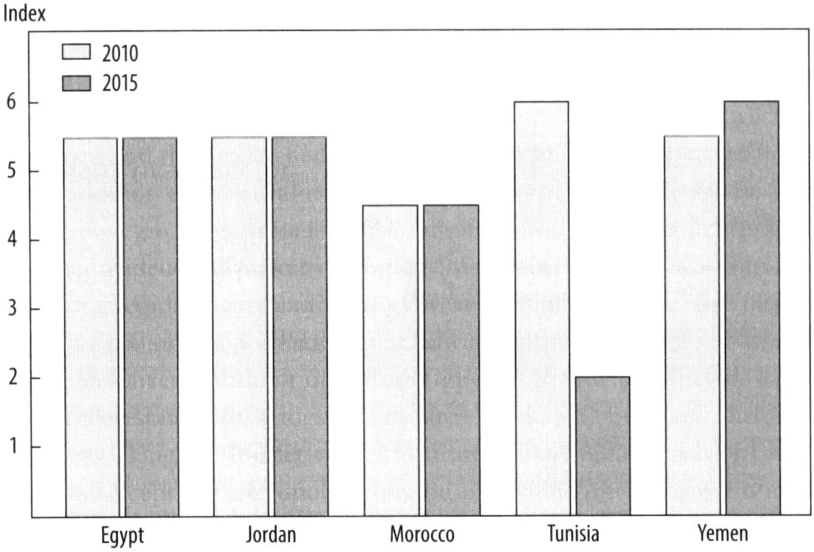

Source: Freedom House.

public support for the evolutionary process, while at the same time avoiding abrupt changes that could result in instability and disruption.

The Arab Spring's Disappointing Political and Economic Results

From the review of country experiences presented above one cannot expect the Arab Spring to have resulted in much improvement in terms of greater democracy and freedom, except maybe in Tunisia. And this is exactly what the Freedom House data, comparing results from 2010 and 2015, presented in figure 2-1, show. Egypt and Jordan, which were rated as not free with a freedom index of 5.5 in 2010, continue with the exact same rating and index level in 2015.[14] Similarly, Morocco's rating as partly free and its index of 4.5 in 2010 remain unchanged in 2015. Yemen's freedom rating actually deteriorated, moving from 5.5 to 6.0.

14. The freedom index is an average of an index for political freedom and one for civil liberties. It goes from 1.0, which is the best rating, indicating greatest freedom, to 6.0, which is least free.

TABLE 2-2. Index of Political Stability and Lack of Violence, Arab Countries in Transition, 2010 and 2013[a]

Country	2010	2013
Egypt	(0.91)	(1.62)
Jordan	(0.31)	(0.62)
Morocco	(0.38)	(0.50)
Tunisia	(0.04)	(0.91)
Yemen	(2.42)	(2.35)

Source: World Bank, Worldwide Governance Indicators.
a. Negative values in parentheses.

Does this mean that the Arab Spring has had no impact on freedom in those countries? Not exactly. Tunisia moved from a rating of 6.0 and a classification of not free to a rating of 2.0, which means that it is now classified as free. That is a great achievement for Tunisia, and it also provides an example for other Arab countries. Tunisia has shown that it is possible to move toward greater freedom and democracy in spite of the secular-Islamist divide, the lack of a democratic tradition and culture, weak or nonexistent institutions.

In all five countries the Arab Spring was associated with an increase in political instability, terrorism, and violence. Table 2-2 presents the index on political stability and absence of violence and terrorism from the Worldwide Governance Indicators. This indicator moves from –2.5 (most unstable) to +2.5 (most stable). Note that all five countries had a negative index in 2010. This means that even before the Arab Spring the five countries were in the relatively unstable range. The situation worsened after the revolutions, and the indexes became more negative for all countries except Yemen. The index for 2014 has not been published yet. However, one can guess that, with the Houthi capture of Sana'a, the counterattacks, the activities of AQAP, and the Saudi-led military intervention, Yemen's index for 2014 will probably show further deterioration.

There seems to be a difference between the republics and the monarchies in the group. While the level of instability increased in the two monarchies, they ended up in 2013 being more stable than any of the three republics. For example, compare Jordan's –0.62 with Egypt's –1.62 or Morocco's –0.50 with Tunisia's –0.91, or compare them both with Yemen's –2.35.

TABLE 2-3. GDP Growth Rates, Arab Countries in Transition, 2010–14[a]

Percent

Country	2010	2011	2012	2013	2014
Egypt	5.1	1.8	2.2	2.1	2.2
Jordan	2.3	2.6	2.7	2.9	3.5
Morocco	3.7	5.0	2.7	4.4	3.5
Tunisia	3.0	(1.9)	3.7	2.3	2.4
Yemen	7.7	(12.7)	2.4	4.8	1.9

Source: International Monetary Fund.
a. Negative values in parentheses.

More violence and instability is obviously not conducive to economic growth and development.[15] Table 2-3 presents real GDP growth for the five countries for the period 2010–14. In 2010 the Arab economies were starting to recover from the impact of the global financial crisis, but with the instability brought about by the revolutions, GDP growth soon fell again. For example, Egypt was growing at 5 percent a year before the Arab Spring but saw its growth fall to about 2 percent the following year. Tunisia and Yemen even saw their GDP slip into negative growth in the year following the revolutions. The two monarchies seem to have done a little better than the three republics, with growth rates of 3.5 percent in 2014.

Low growth was associated with increasing unemployment. By 2014 the unemployment rate had reached 13.4 percent in Egypt and 9.3 percent in Morocco. Youth unemployment in Tunisia rose to 36.4 percent. Paradoxically, revolutions that were started by youth who demanded better job opportunities (in addition to freedom, justice, and dignity) ended up, at least initially, creating more unemployment and worse living conditions.

The four years following the Arab revolutions witnessed increasing fiscal imbalances in all five countries (see table 2-4). This happened because governments tried to jump-start GDP growth by increasing public spending, and at the same time they had to give in to political pressures and provide increased benefits to different groups. Thus

15. For a detailed discussion of macroeconomic developments in Egypt and Tunisia, see Ghanem and Shaikh (2013).

TABLE 2-4. Budget Balance as Share of GDP, Arab Countries in Transition, 2010–14[a]

Percent

Country	2010	2011	2012	2013	2014
Egypt	(8.2)	(9.8)	(10.6)	(13.7)	(11.9)
Jordan	(7.7)	(11.7)	(10.4)	(13.7)	(15.6)
Morocco	(4.6)	(6.9)	(7.4)	(6.2)	(6.3)
Tunisia	(1.1)	(3.5)	(5.7)	(6.2)	(6.4)
Yemen	(4.0)	(5.7)	(12.4)	(7.8)	(6.8)

Source: International Monetary Fund.
a. Negative values in parentheses.

Tunisia's fiscal deficit, which was only 1.1 percent of GDP in 2010, grew nearly sixfold to reach 6.4 percent of GDP in 2014. Egypt and Jordan already had high deficits of 8.2 and 7.7 percent of GDP, respectively, before the Arab Spring. Those deficits ballooned to about 12 and 15.6 percent of GDP in 2014. Yemen had a deficit of 4 percent of GDP in 2010; it rose to more than 12 percent of GDP in 2012. Even Morocco saw its fiscal deficit rise, from 4.6 percent of GDP in 2010 to 7.4 percent in 2012 and 6.3 percent in 2014.

High budget deficits led to big increases in public debt between 2010 and 2014 in all five countries (see figure 2-2). Egypt's public debt rose from 73 percent of GDP in 2010 to nearly 94 percent in 2014, and Jordan's debt rose from 67 to 90 percent of GDP in the same period. Increased government borrowing led to higher interest rates and crowded out private investment. This was particularly true because in most countries, notably Egypt and Jordan, most of the borrowing was done domestically. In Egypt, external debt only increased from 12.4 percent of GDP to 18.4 percent, and in Jordan from 24.6 percent to 30 percent of GDP during the same period. This means that most of the increased government borrowing was happening in the domestic market; between 2010 and 2014, Egypt's domestic debt rose from about 60 percent of GDP to 75 percent, while Jordan's domestic debt rose from about 42 percent of GDP to 60 percent.

Governments were sucking liquidity from domestic banking systems and leaving very little to the private sector. At some point in 2012 domestic interest rates in Egypt were 16 percent at a time when international rates were close to zero. It is therefore no surprise that private

FIGURE 2-2. Public Debt as Share of GDP, Arab Countries in Transition, 2010 and 2014

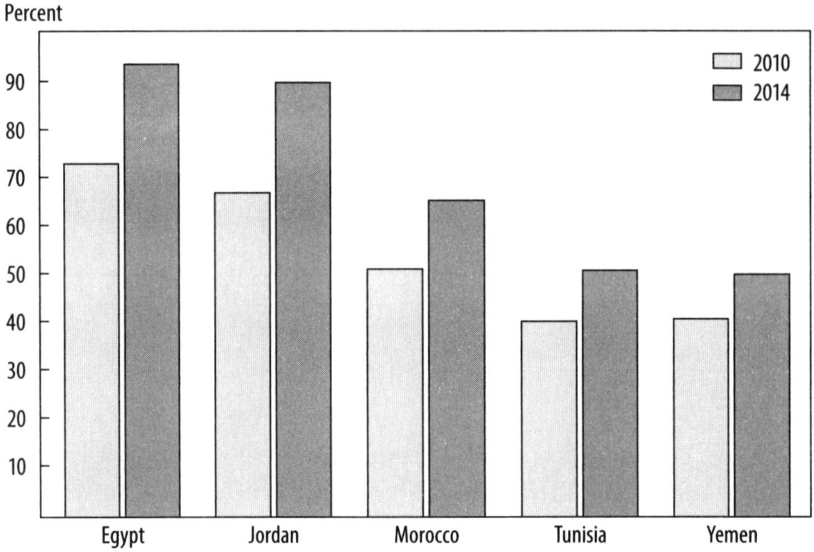

Percent

Source: International Monetary Fund.

investment, and hence growth and job creation, slowed down. High interest rates, together with political uncertainty and civil strife, were a strong disincentive for economic activity.

Two or three years into the transition, governments in all five countries started dealing with their budget problem; they quickly discovered that they must reduce or even eliminate some subsidies, especially those on energy products. In 2012 Tunisia spent about 4 percent of GDP on subsidies, and Egypt spent close to 9 percent of GDP. The Egyptian government allocated about 6–7 percent of GDP on fuel subsidies and some 2 percent of GDP on food subsidies. Combined, they were roughly equal to the entire sum the government (including health and education ministries) paid in wages and salaries and more than double the amount the government invested in infrastructure.

Two other arguments were made against fuel subsidies. First, they encourage the overconsumption of energy, which has environmental as well as economic implications. The energy intensity of the Egyptian economy is estimated to be 2.5–3.0 times higher than the average for advanced countries. Second, it is argued that fuel subsidies are regressive in nature. In Egypt, most subsidy benefits are captured by the richest two-fifths of the income distribution. In Tunisia, the households with the highest income benefit about forty times more from energy subsidies than the poorest households.

Nevertheless, removing subsidies is unpopular and politically difficult. Morocco succeeded in removing all fuel subsidies without much political opposition. Tunisia also reduced fuel subsidies in spite of some opposition. In Egypt, President el-Sissi used the honeymoon period right after his election to reduce subsidies. In Jordan, subsidy reduction was met with street demonstrations. In Yemen, the demonstrations against subsidy cuts paved the way for the Houthi invasion of Sana'a.

The present crisis should lead to a rethinking of Arab policies on price subsidies and social policies in general. It is time for Arab countries to overhaul their archaic safety-net system and develop a new social contract that reflects the realities of the twenty-first century.

Over the past two decades, many middle-income countries (for example, Brazil and Mexico) shifted to social protection systems based on targeted cash transfers, but Arab countries maintained their system based on generalized price subsidies. This is the system adopted by President Nasser in Egypt more than fifty years ago, and it involves subsidizing prices of a number of commodities (including fuel, electricity, bread, rice, edible oil, tea, and sugar).

Social protection based on generalized price subsidies may or may not have worked in the 1960s, but it is certainly not working now. Generalized price subsidies are part of what has come to be known as the autocratic bargain or the autocratic social contract. This has included free health care and education, government jobs for all graduates, and low prices for necessities but limited political and civil liberties. The Arab Spring revolutions demonstrated the limits of that arrangement and highlighted the need to develop a new social contract—one that is consistent with a market economy and responds to youth demands for freedom, dignity, and social justice.

The idea of putting in place a social protection system based on targeted cash transfers has been studied in the Arab world for several years and could be quickly implemented. Experience from around the world indicates that such a system is much less expensive, more efficient, and fairer than price subsidies. Arab governments should consider moving ahead quickly to put such a system in place. It makes economic as well as political sense. It would be one way of responding to demands

TABLE 2-5. International Reserves, by Months of Imports, Arab Countries in Transition, 2010–14

Country	2010	2011	2012	2013	2014
Egypt	6.9	4.7	2.7	2.5	2.7
Jordan	7.4	5.9	3.6	5.1	5.8
Morocco	5.7	5.0	4.2	4.3	4.5
Tunisia	4.4	3.4	3.9	3.4	3.6
Yemen	6.0	3.9	5.6	4.6	3.6

Source: International Monetary Fund.

for greater social justice, and it would make implementation of future reforms and further subsidy reductions much easier.

Political instability in the Arab world was also associated with a deterioration in external accounts. Tourism declined, foreign direct investment fell, and capital flight increased. The result has been a fall in foreign reserves (table 2-5). The decline in Egypt's foreign reserves has been the most marked, as they fell from the equivalent of about 6.9 months of imports in 2010 to only 2.7 months of imports in 2014, which is slightly less than the three months that are usually considered the minimum prudential requirement. As shown in table 2-5, the other four countries also experienced significant declines in their reserve covers, though not as dramatic as that experienced by Egypt.

As a result, the credit ratings of all of the Arab countries in transition (ACTs) suffered. In 2010 Tunisia's debt was rated by Moody's as Baa, which means that it was considered medium grade and subject to moderate risk. In early 2015 it is rated as Ba, which means that it is speculative and subject to substantial risk. Egypt's debt was rated as Ba before the Arab Spring and is rated as Caa in 2015, which means that it is now of poor standing and subject to very high credit risk. Jordan also saw its credit rating deteriorate from Ba to B, meaning that it is considered a high credit risk.

The decline in credit rating and increased sovereign risk make it more difficult for the private sector to engage in international business, particularly to obtain credit on the international market. This complicates international trade and makes it more difficult for the country to import. Some Egyptian businessmen complained to me in 2013 that it took about six weeks to open a letter of credit to import goods, while it took only three days before the revolution.

Increased Fragility and Risks Going Forward

Where are the ACTs heading? Are they moving toward more chaos, terrorism, and civil strife, or are they going to succeed in building stable and prosperous democracies? The jury is still out on this question. However, it seems clear that the ACTs are facing serious risks going forward. In the Arab world today, Yemen, Syria, and Libya are looking more and more like failed states. Will others follow them?

Yemen presents a worst-case scenario in which the dreams of liberty and better living standards have turned into a nightmare of civil war, increasing tribalism and sectarianism, escalating terrorism, lack of human rights, increasing poverty, and greater injustice. The country seems to have entered into a vicious circle where frustration over the lack of concrete political and economic results from the 2011 revolution lead to civil unrest, which, in turn, leads to more violence and repression and even worse economic and social conditions. Yemen seems to have become a failed state that could break up into two or more entities at any time.

Tunisia is probably the best-case scenario. After four long years the country's political elite was able to reach a historic compromise on a constitution and to carry out free and fair elections whose results were accepted by all parties. The Tunisian political forces were also able to agree on a broad coalition government that includes Islamists as well as secularists. Therefore, it seems that Tunisia is on its way to meeting the revolution's demands for freedom and democracy while maintaining political stability and national unity.

But Tunisia's impressive achievements are still fragile, and the country remains vulnerable to extremism and violence. It is threatened by terrorism from groups who continue to dream of turning Tunisia into a theocracy. Ansar al-Sharia is a Tunisian terrorist group that was created in 2011. It is suspected of having been behind the attacks on the American embassy and the American School in 2012. It is also suspected of assassinating two secular political figures, Chokri Belaid and Mohammed al-Brahimi, in 2013. Al-Qaeda in the Islamic Maghreb has also been operating in Tunisia since 2011, particularly targeting security personnel. For example, on July 16, 2014, fourteen Tunisian soldiers were killed and more than twenty were injured during a terrorist attack on Mount Chaambi, a closed military zone where the Tunisian army has been tracking terrorist groups since the end of 2012. In 2015 the Bardo museum and Sousse attacks were crucial blows to tourism. Moreover, significant numbers of Tunisian youth are in Syria fighting with extremist groups, such as the Islamic State. How will those young men fit into Tunisian society when they return?

Building national consensus in Egypt has proved to be more difficult than in Tunisia. The year during which the Muslim Brotherhood was in power has left deep marks on the Egyptian body politic, and hardly anyone is willing to restart a dialogue with the Brotherhood to work toward national reconciliation. Moreover, there is a divide among secular politicians, and many of the democracy activists who led the 2011 revolution feel excluded from current political processes.

Egypt has been plagued by terrorist attacks—mostly targeting government officials, Coptic Christians, and tourists—for many decades.[16] But the number and intensity of those attacks increased dramatically after the ouster of Mohamed Morsi in July 2013. According to government sources, more than five hundred soldiers, police officers, and civilians have been killed in terrorist attacks since 2013.[17] Perhaps the greatest terrorist challenge has been in the Sinai Peninsula, where the group Ansar Beit al-Maqdis, which has recently sworn allegiance to the organization of the Islamic State, has been active attacking army and police installations and personnel. It also claimed responsibility for an assassination attempt against the minister of interior, for attacks on police headquarters in Cairo, Ismailia, Dakahlia, and Sharqiya, and for a suicide attack against a tour bus of Korean tourists near Taba. As the security forces focused their efforts on curbing activities of Ansar Beit al-Maqdis in Sinai, smaller attacks on police checkpoints and individuals in Egypt's urban centers have continued.

---

16. Nearly all the terrorist groups operating in Egypt since the 1970s have been inspired by the work of Sayyid Qutb, a Muslim Brotherhood leader who was executed in 1966 after an assassination attempt against President Nasser. Qutb's most famous book (*Maalim Fi al-Tariq*, translated into English as *Milestones*) is a manifesto for armed jihad to bring about the kingdom of God on earth (Qutb 1990).

17. For more on the terrorism data in Egypt, see Gold (2014).

The two monarchies have so far been more stable than the republics, but they too face some challenges and risks. Ethnic differences between Transjordanians and Palestinians in Jordan or between Berbers and Arabs in Morocco represent an important challenge to national unity. Moreover, both monarchies, but especially Jordan, have to deal with important external threats. They are both situated in dangerous neighborhoods.

The crisis in Syria has had direct impacts on Jordan, which has received 600,000 registered refugees and an estimated 1.3 million refugees in all.[18] Jordan's population is about 7 million, which means that Syrian refugees represent more than 15 percent of the population. Imagine if the United States had to receive 57 million foreign refugees. In relative terms this is what Jordan is dealing with, and obviously it has economic, social, and political implications. But there are other crises on Jordan's borders. The crisis in Iraq has impacted Jordan's economy because Iraq is Jordan's main export market, receiving more than 18 percent of Jordanian exports.[19] Moreover, the Israeli-Palestinian conflict directly impacts Jordan because of its long borders with the West Bank and its large population of Palestinian origin.

Morocco is also impacted but to a lesser extent, given its geographical location. Moroccan officials estimate that there are more than one thousand Moroccans fighting with jihadist groups in Iraq and Syria. In July 2014 they announced a tightening of security measures for fear that returning jihadist fighters would carry out attacks on Moroccan soil or use Morocco as a launching pad for terrorist attacks on other countries. In addition, the group al-Qaeda in the Islamic Maghreb operates in neighboring Algeria and in the Sahel. Reports that the group is working with the Polisario Front, which rejects Morocco's sovereignty over the Western Sahara, are cause for concern as they indicate additional risks of attacks against Morocco.[20]

---

18. Some observers estimate the total number of Syrian refugees in Jordan at 1.3 million; see "Syrian Refugee Crisis in Jordan Tests Hospitality," *BBC News*, February 2, 2015.

19. See International Monetary Fund (2014).

20. For example, see Le Polisario aux cotés d'AQMI au Mali," Sahel Intelligence, March 1, 2013.

The Need for Action on the Economy

It is obvious from the preceding discussion that building stable democracies in the Arab world will require action on the security and political fronts. This has been the focus of Arab governments and their foreign partners. In Yemen, Syria, Iraq, and Libya the international community has focused on supporting negotiations and national dialogues while also strengthening security arrangements and waging a war against terrorist groups like the Islamic State of Iraq and Syria, al-Qaeda in the Arabian Peninsula in Yemen, or al-Qaeda in the Islamic Maghreb in North Africa. It appears that there has been a decision, conscious or otherwise, to postpone dealing with economic and social issues, except for relief operations for refugees and displaced people, until the political and security situation is stabilized. I believe that this is a mistake.

Peace and stability—and hence successful transitions to democracy—cannot be achieved as long as large segments of the population suffer from economic and social exclusion. Hence an economic program to achieve inclusive growth—together with actions on the political and security fronts—should be an integral part of any policy package that aims at building stable and prosperous democracies in the Arab world.

To be credible, and to attract widespread support for the political process, such an economic program needs to be broad enough to touch large segments of Arab society. The countries of the Arab region are facing similar threats, and therefore it would make sense for them to cooperate on developing a regional program for inclusive growth.

3

Roots of the Arab Spring

Anyone following Arab or international media today would think that the Arab uprisings of 2010–11 were all about political issues, and particularly about defining national identity. As highlighted in chapter 1, the Arab world seems to be divided between secularists and Islamists, Muslims and Christians, Sunnis and Shia, jihadists and spiritualists, liberal democrats and militant nationalists, and so on. Economic issues have been put on the back burner. The revolutions' demands for more bread and greater social justice have been forgotten.

This chapter argues that economic issues were at the heart of the Arab Spring. It is true that Arab economies had solid growth rates during the decade preceding the uprisings. However, that growth was not inclusive. The middle class was squeezed, youth were left out, women were pushed out of the labor market, and many regions (for example, Upper Egypt and western Tunisia) were marginalized. Limited economic opportunities and increasing inequality were key drivers of the Arab Spring.

Arab Economies Were Growing before the Revolutions

The so-called Arab countries in transition (ACTs) experienced respectable growth rates over the period 1991–2010 (table 3-1). This was especially true at the beginning of the twenty-first century—that is, in the ten years immediately preceding the revolutions of late 2010 and early 2011. As table 3-1 shows, Egypt's growth rates during 2000–10 were in the range of 4–6 percent and Jordan's in the range of 6–7 percent, while Morocco, Tunisia, and Yemen were growing at around 4.5 percent a year.

TABLE 3-1. Average GDP Growth Rate, ACTs, 1991–2010

Percent

Country	1991–94	1995–99	2000–04	2005–10
Egypt	2.4	5.8	3.9	5.9
Jordan	6.4	3.6	5.6	6.6
Morocco	3.1	2.3	4.7	4.6
Tunisia	4.6	5.2	4.5	4.4
Yemen	6.3	5.1	4.3	4.6

Source: Data from International Monetary Fund, *World Economic Outlook*. Author's calculations.

How do these growth rates compare with those of the rest of the world, and were the ACTs' income levels converging? It depends. Table 3-2 shows that ACT income levels, compared with U.S. levels, have been converging since the late 1990s but at a snail's pace. On the other hand, compared with India and especially with China, it is significant divergence.

Table 3-2 shows the ratio of per capita GDP (in trend-purchasing-power-parity dollars) in the ACTs to U.S. per capita GDP, and it also includes three of the four emerging economies known as BRICs (Brazil, China, and India) for comparison.[1] The table shows that the 1980s and 1990s were a period of divergence for most countries, including the ACTs.[2] The ratio for Brazil fell from 37 percent in 1980 to 28 percent in 1990 and to 24 percent in 2000. India remained stagnant in the 1980s at 5 percent of U.S. GDP. During the 1980s, per capita GDP in Jordan, Morocco, and Tunisia fell relative to the United States, while Egypt's per capita GDP remained more or less unchanged in relative terms, moving from 17 to 18 percent of U.S. levels. China is a clear exception to this trend, as the ratio of Chinese to U.S. per capita GDP doubled, from 2 to 4 percent, in the 1980s and doubled again in the 1990s to 8 percent.

The situation began to change in the 1990s and especially the early years of this century as most emerging and developing economies, including the ACTs, started converging toward income levels of Organization for Economic Cooperation and Development (OECD) countries. Egypt's

1. The fourth is Russia. The analysis was also done using per capita GDP in nominal terms and gross national income in nominal as well as in purchasing-power-parity terms. The conclusions do not change.

2. For more, see Pritchett (1997).

TABLE 3-2. Ratio of per Capita GDP to U.S. per Capita GDP, in TPPP Dollars, ACTs and BRICs, 1980–2013[a]

Percent

Country	1980	1990	2000	2010	2013
Brazil	37	28	24	28	28
China	2	4	8	19	22
India	5	5	6	9	10
Egypt	17	18	18	22	21
Jordan	29	18	17	23	22
Morocco	12	11	10	13	14
Tunisia	17	15	16	21	21
Yemen	n.a.	9	8	9	7

Source: Data from International Monetary Fund, *World Economic Outlook*. Author's calculations.
a. TPPP = trend purchasing power parity.

and Jordan's GDP per capita, which were 18 percent of U.S. GDP in 1990, rose to 22 and 23 percent, respectively, by 2010. During the same period Morocco moved from 11 to 13 percent of U.S. GDP, and Tunisia from 15 to 21 percent. However, the growth rates of convergence are very slow. At those rates Jordan would catch up with the United States somewhere around 2060, Tunisia would catch up around 2070, Morocco around 2080, and Egypt around 2090. Yemen shows virtually no convergence. Moreover, political upheaval after 2010 has led to a slowdown in the ACT economies, implying slower convergence in general and even an outright return to divergence in Egypt, Jordan, and Yemen.

Emerging economies, especially India and China, have been growing at much faster rates and therefore converging much faster to OECD levels. This also means that the ACTs are rapidly losing ground compared with those economies. In 1980 Jordan's GDP per capita was 647 percent that of India, and Tunisia's was 374 percent; by 2013 those ratios had fallen to 214 percent and 202 percent, respectively.[3] At this rate India's per capita GDP will surpass that of nearly all ACTs before the end of the century.

The comparison with China is even more dramatic. In 1980 Egypt's GDP per capita was more than seven times that of China, whereas

3. Data from IMF, *World Economic Outlook*. Author's calculations.

now it is 10 percent lower in purchasing-power-parity terms. Today, Yemen's GDP per capita is about one-third that of China. It is hard to believe that in 1990 Yemen had a GDP per capita that was more than double that of China.

Nevertheless, with the exception of Yemen, the ACTs' growth rates were sufficient to bring about significant reductions in extreme poverty. By 2010, $2-a-day poverty was nearly eliminated in Jordan and was cut by three-fourths in Tunisia and by nearly half in Egypt. Morocco went through a big increase in poverty in the 1990s and then a huge decline from 2000 to 2010, which I find hard to explain.[4]

Yet Arabs Were Dissatisfied

The Arab revolutions of 2010–11 took everybody by surprise. However, with the benefit of hindsight, it now appears that analysts and specialists of the region should have seen it coming. The mood in the Arab world was gloomy in spite of the good economic results.

Figure 3-1 shows data from the World Values Survey for the period just before the Arab revolutions, that is, wave 5 of the survey. I present data for the four Arab countries that participated in this wave plus four other middle-income countries that are used as comparators. Iraq is clearly an outlier, with more than 45 percent of respondents stating that they were both dissatisfied with their lives and unhappy. Given what was happening in Iraq at the time (and continues to happen today), can anyone really blame them?

But even excluding Iraq, the other three Arab countries' level of dissatisfaction and unhappiness seems to have been very high relative to the comparators. More than 30 percent of Egyptians said that they were dissatisfied with their lives. Compare that with about 6 percent of Brazilians, 8 percent of Malaysians, 10 percent of Indonesians, and 19 percent of Indians. Looking at the proportion of people who said they were not happy yields similar results, except that India appears to be an outlier. The Arab countries have much higher unhappiness numbers than Brazil, Indonesia, and Malaysia.

---

4. World Bank, World Development Indicators. Data from the household survey closest to the year in question.

FIGURE 3-1. Dissatisfaction and Unhappiness among Surveyed ACT Respondents

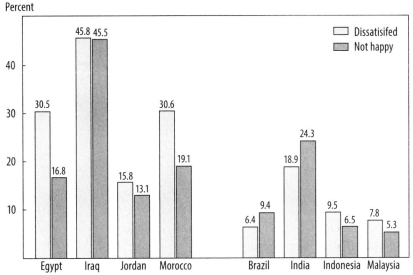

Source: Data from World Values Survey, wave 5 (2005–09). Period covered by country: Egypt 2008, Iraq 2006, Jordan 2007, Morocco 2007, Brazil 2006, India 2006, Indonesia 2006, Malaysia 2006.

It is important to understand why the Arabs revolted in 2010–11, because failure to respond to the demands expressed by Arab youth during that time could imply political and social instability over the medium term and, in some cases, the collapse of nation states and widespread civil strife. It sometimes appears as if today's political leaders have not yet fully internalized the lessons of the Arab Spring, which does not augur well for future economic and social developments.

There are three possible explanations for the Arab revolutions: the revolts were against political circumstances and had nothing to do with economic conditions; economic growth in the ACTs was not inclusive, and large segments of the population, especially youth, were left out; and the revolts reflected dissatisfaction with both the political and the economic conditions in those countries.

Explanations for the Arab Revolutions

Some of the proponents of the view that the revolts were only political point to the data shown in table 3-3, which indicate that all the ACTs

TABLE 3-3. Governance Scores for 2010 (percentile rank)

Country	Voice and accountability	Political stability	Government effectiveness	Regulatory quality	Rule of law	Control of corruption
Egypt	13.7	19.3	43.1	46.9	51.2	34.3
Jordan	27.5	34.4	59.3	57.4	61.1	60.9
Morocco	28.9	33.0	50.7	51.2	50.2	53.3
Tunisia	10.0	44.3	63.2	53.1	59.7	54.8
Yemen	10.9	1.9	14.3	30.1	13.3	10.0

Source: World Bank, Worldwide Governance Indicators.

had low governance scores. Their lowest scores were in the area of voice and accountability, where the five Arab countries fell in the bottom one-third of all developing countries. And Tunisia, where the Arab Spring started, fell in the bottom 10 percent. It is argued that with economic development and higher living standards people typically start demanding more voice in the management of national affairs, and that is what the Arab revolts were all about.

According to this view, Arab countries were simply following in the footsteps of more advanced East Asian (for example, South Korea) and Latin American (for example, Brazil) countries, where economic development and an expansion of education led to greater demands for political and civil liberties and ultimately the fall of long-ruling autocratic regimes. In the case of the Arab countries, the process may have been accelerated by the revolution in information technology, and particularly the expansion of social media, which were used by revolutionary youth to organize and mobilize support.

Of course, there are also the conspiracy theorists. Some proponents of the politics-only explanation of the revolutions claim that they were the result of an international conspiracy. They point to the chaotic state in which Arab countries that went through revolutions find themselves today and the explosion of ethnic and sectarian conflicts all around the region following the Arab Spring. They conclude that the revolutions of 2010–11 were fueled by outside forces that wanted to destroy Arab nation-states and thus maintain the Arab world in a state of perpetual weakness and dependence on foreigners.[5]

5. For an exposition of conspiracy theories see, Abdrabo (2015).

Most Western observers, and some Arabs, do not take those conspiracy theories seriously. After all it is hard to see how creating chaos in the Middle East and North Africa, with the ensuing wars, exodus of refugees, increasing terrorism, and large-scale migration movements to Europe, could be in the strategic interest of the great international powers. The Arab world is important, but is it really so important that the world will invest huge resources conspiring to weaken it? Many observers believe that those conspiracy theories are just attempts by the ruling elites to blame foreigners for their own failures.

Nevertheless, it would be a mistake to ignore conspiracy theories simply because they seem so far fetched. This may be a case where perception is more important than reality. Many Arabs appear to subscribe to those theories. The defense of former Egyptian president Hosni Mubarak, in his trial for the killing of young demonstrators by security forces, presented the revolutionaries in Tahrir Square as agents of foreign powers intent on destroying the Egyptian state that President Mubarak was trying so hard to protect.

Most of the conspiracy theories are somehow linked to the Arab-Israeli conflict. The argument supporting the idea of a global conspiracy against the Arab nations is quite simple, maybe even simplistic. It is based on the premise that ensuring Israel's security is a key Western, and especially U.S., priority. Therefore, it is argued, the West is always conspiring to keep the Arabs weak in order to protect Israel.

The conspiracy argument is not very convincing. The United States and its Western allies do not need to destabilize a whole region, support jihadist ideologies, and support global terrorism to ensure Israel's security. They have sufficient technical, economic, and military superiority to do that, while avoiding the human and economic costs associated with fragile or failed Arab states and increasing terrorist attacks around the world.

Nevertheless, failure to resolve the Arab-Israeli conflict seems to complicate Arab transition to democracy. The conflict provides arguments that support extremist ideologies and conspiracy theories. Israel's military superiority (achieved with Western help), its failure to acknowledge Palestinian rights, and the daily humiliations that Arabs endure at the hands of Israeli security forces create a feeling of victimization. As a result, Arab societies have become more accepting of violence, more suspicious of foreigners, and more willing to sacrifice liberty on the altar of national security and the struggle against the Israeli occupiers.

It Is the Economy after All

Even if the conspiracy theorists were right and foreign powers were supporting the revolutions, it is hard to imagine that masses of young people would have taken to the streets of Tunis, Cairo, and Sana'a if they did not have real grievances. The revolutionaries called for bread, freedom, social justice, and human dignity. That is, the slogans of the revolutions included economic (bread and social justice) as well as political (freedom and human dignity) demands. But the slogan that attracted most attention was "The people want the fall of the regime." As stated in the previous chapter, there is a difference between the so-called Arab republics (Egypt, Tunisia, and Yemen) and the monarchies (Jordan and Morocco). The people of Egypt, Tunisia, and Yemen demanded regime change, while those of Jordan and Morocco demanded changes in the existing regime. It seems that monarchs enjoy a greater sense of legitimacy than authoritarian presidents in the Arab world.

The hypothesis that Arabs revolted only for political reasons is not supported by available data. After the revolution, Arab Barometer conducted a survey asking Tunisians to state the main reason for their revolt. Figure 3-2 presents the results. About 63 percent of respondents said that the weak economy was the main reason behind the revolution. This may appear surprising at first sight, since, as shown earlier, Tunisian economic performance (measured in terms of real growth) was not weak before the revolution. However, it may be the case that many Tunisians did not benefit from growth. They were left out, and hence from their perspective the economy was weak.

The second reason given for the revolutions, high levels of corruption, could also be considered economic. Some 17 percent of Tunisians said that corruption was the main driver for the revolution. Of course, corruption is not a purely economic problem. In the case of Tunisia (and Egypt), large-scale corruption reflected a special relationship between political and economic elites, whereby some large businesses were supported by political elites and hence received special privileges and protection.

FIGURE 3-2. Tunisians' Reasons for Revolting against President Ben Ali

Percent

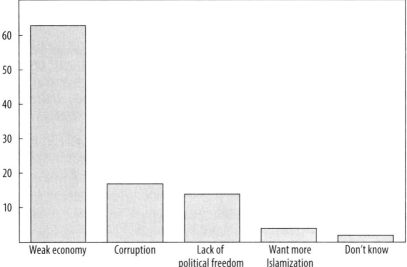

Source: Arab Barometer survey, wave 3 (2012–14).

Only 14 percent of Tunisians said that they revolted because of lack of political freedom. More strikingly, a mere 4 percent of Tunisians said that they revolted because they wanted to live in a more Islamic society.

The emphasis on economic issues does not mean that Arabs do not care for democracy. In survey after survey Arabs have repeated their strong belief in democracy. The latest wave of the World Values Survey (2010–14) highlights that nearly 99 percent of Egyptians, 86 percent of Jordanians and Tunisians, 85 percent of Moroccans, and 80 percent of Yemenis said that democracy is the preferred form of government.

If democracy is so popular in the Arab world, why is democracy having such a difficult time taking hold? Egyptian president el-Sissi shed some light on this question in a paper he wrote in 2006 while he was attending the U.S. Army War College. In this paper he describes the constraints on democracy in the Arab world, namely poverty, lack of a democratic culture, religious extremism, Arab-Israeli conflict, and the negative perception Arabs have of the West, particularly the United States. He clearly sees democratization as a long-term process. El-Sissi states,

It is one thing to say that democracy is a preferred form of government, but quite another to adjust to its requirements and
accept some [of] the risks that go along with it. . . . The economic,
religious, education, media, security and legal systems will be
affected. As a result, it will take time for people and the nation's
systems to adjust to the new form of government. . . . In my opinion democracy needs [a] good environment like a reasonable economic situation, educated people and a moderate understanding
of religious issues.[6]

According to el-Sissi, to develop democracy in the Middle East four
things need to happen. First, the education system should be strengthened and the media should play a bigger role in spreading a culture of
democracy. Second, a consensus needs to be reached on the appropriate
role of religion in government. Third, there needs to be greater regional
integration and exchange of lessons and experiences. Fourth, as the
Middle East develops, the rest of the world needs to assist in promoting
democratic values, perhaps by supporting education.

Finally, it is important to note that Arabs support democracy for
economic as well as political reasons. Table 3-4 shows the results
from the World Values Survey for the question concerning the essential characteristics of democracy. Unsurprisingly, the ability to choose
one's leaders through free elections received the most votes as an
essential characteristic of democracy. However, neither protection of
civil liberties nor equal rights for women ranked second. The second
most commonly cited characteristic of democracy, according to Arab
respondents, is that governments provide unemployment benefits. In
Morocco, more people picked unemployment insurance as an essential characteristic of democracy than free elections. According to this
survey, the third most important characteristic of democracy is that
governments tax the rich to subsidize the poor. In Jordan, 31 percent
of respondents picked this as an essential characteristic of democracy,
while only 22 percent picked free elections and just 13 percent picked
the protection of civil liberties.

This is not to say that the desire for greater political and civil liberties was not an important driver for the Arab Spring. I am only pointing

---

6. El-Sissi (2006, pp. 2–3).

TABLE 3-4. Respondents' View of Essential Characteristics of Democracy

Country	Government taxing rich to subsidize poor	Government providing unemployment benefits	State equalizing people's incomes	Free elections	Protection of civil liberties	Equal rights for women
Egypt	25.3	24.4	27.4	45.4	27.7	24.7
Jordan	30.9	20.3	8.8	21.7	12.9	17.5
Morocco	36.2	52.7	37.2	50.1	39.1	46.4
Tunisia	30.0	40.2	22.1	47.1	41.9	36.4
Yemen	47.9	41.8	31.3	69.1	38.3	42.0

Source: World Values Survey, wave 6 (2010–14). Periods covered by country: Egypt 2012, Jordan 2014, Morocco 2011, Tunisia 2013, Yemen 2013.

out that polling data indicate that economic factors may have been even more important drivers. The data from Tunisia, the first Arab Spring country, show that while 63 percent of Tunisians felt that the weak economy was the main cause of the revolution, only 14 percent said the same about lack of political freedom (see figure 3-2). Moreover, while huge majorities of Arabs believe that democracy is the preferred political system, most of them seem to support democracy because they believe that it would bring about economic benefits in terms of greater equality and more protection for the poor and vulnerable.

The Middle Class Felt Left Out

Recent research has stressed the important role the middle class plays in economic development.[7] The middle class is seen as important for the political stability that is necessary for economic growth. It is also a source of entrepreneurship and new ideas that are necessary for the small businesses that fuel the world's economy. Middle-class values also emphasize education and savings. Thus the middle class is a key source of investment in human and physical capital. Finally, the middle class represents the most important source of demand for consumer goods and services, and therefore it is an important driver of development for domestic industries.

7. For example see Kharas (2010) or Banerjee and Duflo (2008).

TABLE 3-5. Share of the Population That Is Middle Class, using the Kharas Definition
Percent

Country	1990	2000	2010
Egypt	7.7	11.3	22.4
Jordan	11.7	15.8	36.0
Morocco	5.7	6.2	10.7
Tunisia	15.7	25.5	41.1
Yemen	1.0	2.0	2.0
Brazil	24.7	31.0	45.2
China	0.0	2.0	12.0
India	1.0	1.0	5.0

Source: Brookings database.

There are several definitions of the middle class. I use two different definitions to test the robustness of my conclusions. I start by using the definition developed by Kharas (2010), who defines the global middle class as those people who live on $10–100 per capita per day in purchasing-power-parity terms. He calculates the size of the middle class separately for 145 countries, using distributional parameters from household surveys and adjusting the mean of the distribution to reflect the consumption level from the national income accounts. I then use the definition developed by Banerjee and Duflo (2008) and define the middle class solely using household surveys, with the middle class comprising people living on $2–10 a day.

Table 3-5 presents the proportion of the population that is in the middle class, according to the Kharas definition, for the five ACTs as well as Brazil, China, and India. It shows that the relative size of the middle class has been increasing gradually in the ACTs and that this increase accelerated in the twenty-first century. In Egypt and Jordan, the relative size of the middle class more than doubled between 2000 and 2010, while in Morocco and Tunisia over the same period it increased by more than 60 percent.

The comparison with Brazil is interesting, because it shows that, except for Tunisia, the ACTs are still far from achieving the level of Brazil, where 45 percent of the population is middle class. In relative terms the Brazilian middle class is more than double that of Egypt and is 25 percent larger than that of Jordan. The comparison with China and India shows the difference in the speed of development of the middle class. During 2000–10 China increased the relative size of its middle class sixfold, while India increased its fivefold. Of course, they both started from a very low base—from where Yemen was ten years ago and where it still is today.

In spite of the increase in the proportion of the population that is middle class in the ACTs, the absolute number of people who are below middle class continued to increase everywhere except in Tunisia. In Egypt, Jordan, and Morocco the number of people below middle class rose from 52.5 million, 3.0 million, and 23.4 million, respectively, in 1990 to 63.0 million, 4.0 million and 28.5 million in 2010. The number of people below middle class in Yemen nearly doubled, from 11.8 to 23.5 million, over the same period. Tunisia has been doing better than the other four Arab countries. Nevertheless, the absolute number of Tunisians living below middle class did not fall significantly and remained around 6 million people.[8] Moreover, those people who were left out tended to be concentrated geographically in the country's interior.[9]

I get similar results using the Banerjee and Duflo definition. Since the lower limit for middle class according to this definition is set quite low at $2 a day, there is no increase in the number of people living below middle class (that is, poor), as described earlier, and, in fact, poverty decreased in the Arab countries before the revolutions. The middle class has grown steadily according to this definition. However, there is an increase in the number of people stuck in lower-middle-class status, consuming between $2 and $6 a day. That is, people did get out of poverty but remained very close to the poverty line. Of course, there are variations by countries. While the number of people stuck in lower-middle-class status increased from 36.5 million in the early 1990s to 57.2 million right before the revolution in Egypt and from 14.4 million to 19 million in Morocco, it remained virtually unchanged at about 4.5 million people in Tunisia during the same period.[10]

Thus I could propose one possible explanation for popular dissatisfaction in the ACTs despite economic growth. The number of people

8. Brookings database, 2010.
9. For more on this point see Boughzala (2013).
10. Data from PovCalNet. Author's calculations.

living below middle class (according to the Kharas definition) or in the lower middle class (according to the Banerjee-Duflo definition) and therefore feeling left out from the benefits of growth has been increasing in absolute terms. There was an increasing group of unhappy citizens willing to go into the streets to express their dissatisfaction and demand what they considered to be their rights.

Of course, one could always argue that with continued strong growth people who are initially left out would have ended up benefiting as the middle class expanded further. This is probably true. However, it is not politically realistic. With the benefit of hindsight, it would probably have made more sense for Arab governments to adopt active policies aimed at expanding the middle class rather than waiting for trickle-down to work.

Youth Felt Excluded

Within the middle class it appears that youth felt more excluded from the benefits of growth than their elders. Conventional wisdom has it that youth unemployment was the main driver of the Arab Spring. There is probably a lot of truth in that, but a careful analysis of the data leads to more nuanced conclusions. Overall, youth unemployment does not appear to be particularly high in the Arab region. But there are three important issues relating to the youth job market. First, female unemployment is exceptionally high and female labor force participation is exceptionally low, which makes it difficult for young couples to create middle-class families with two working adults. Second, unemployment seems to rise with education level, which leads to greater dissatisfaction on the part of unemployed graduates and their families. Third, those who do find jobs are often dissatisfied because they end up finding only precarious and poorly paid employment.

Table 3-6 presents unemployment rates in seven Arab countries and compares them with Indonesia, Malaysia (Muslim-majority countries), Brazil, and South Africa (two BRICs). Looking at the overall youth unemployment rates, it is noted that individual country experiences differ; for example, unemployment rates in Saudi Arabia and in Tunisia are higher than in other Arab countries. At the same time, it is difficult to conclude from these data that youth unemployment is a significantly

TABLE 3-6. Youth Unemployment Rates

Percent

Country	Youth	Male	Female
Arab			
Egypt	24.8	14.7	54.1
Tunisia	29.4	27.8	32.7
Algeria	21.5	18.7	37.6
Syria	20.4	16.4	43.5
Saudi Arabia	30.0	23.5	54.8
Bahrain	5.0	2.5	11.6
Qatar	1.2	0.5	7.0
Comparator			
Indonesia	21.4	21.0	22.0
Malaysia	11.4	11.0	12.0
Brazil	17.8	13.8	23.1
South Africa	50.5	47.2	54.6

Source: International Labor Organization (2010 and 2011).

bigger problem in Arab countries than in the comparators. Youth unemployment appears to be a global problem, not just an Arab one. However, as shown in chapter 5, Arab youth have the lowest labor force participation rate in the world. Hence the unemployment rate may not be a good measure as discouraged youth leave the labor market.

It is clear from table 3-6, that young Arab females face a much more serious unemployment problem than their Arab brothers and certainly a more serious one than their sisters in the comparator countries. A young Egyptian male has a significantly lower probability of being unemployed than a young Indonesian male. However, a young Egyptian female's probability of being unemployed is more than twice as high as that of an Indonesian woman of the same age.

High female unemployment rates are coupled with very low female labor force participation rates. Figure 3-3 plots female labor force participation rates against GDP per capita and shows that the countries of the Middle East and North Africa are clear outliers.

Low female participation rates, together with the high female unemployment rates, mean that only about 18 percent of working-age Arab

FIGURE 3-3. Female Labor Force Participation across Country, 2010

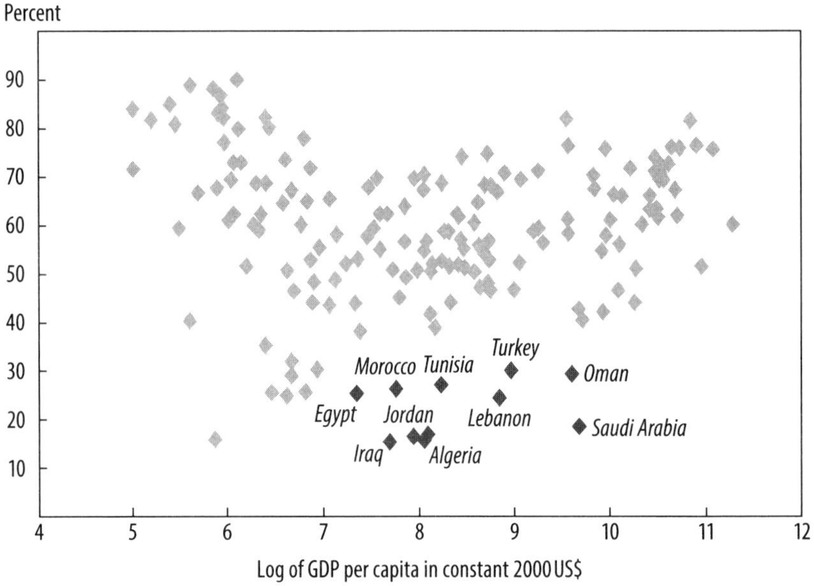

Percent

Log of GDP per capita in constant 2000 US$

Source: Morikawa (2015a).

women actually have jobs.[11] Obviously this implies a waste of resources, especially since many of these women are educated. It also makes it much harder to develop a middle class. Today most middle-class families around the world depend on two breadwinners. This is still not the case in the Arab world, which appears to be stuck in mid-twentieth-century paradigms of family structures and gender roles. That situation would not have been a major problem if productivity and wages in the Arab world were so high that a working man could ensure a middle-class life for his family. But this is not the case.

The result is severe frustration, as young men are unable to earn enough to get married, find a place to live, and raise a family, and young educated women stay at home waiting to get married. As described by Assaad and Barsoum (2007), this has led to a whole generation in waiting: waiting for better jobs, waiting for housing, and waiting to get married and raise a family. Some of the social ills observed in some Arab countries today could probably be explained, at least in part, by this situation.

11. See Steer, Ghanem, and Jalbout (2014).

Being young, educated, and unemployed is a major source of frustration. Boughzala (2013) studies the relationship between education and unemployment in Tunisia, which is quite representative of other Arab countries. He shows that between 2005 and May 2011, the unemployment rate rose from 6.5 percent to 8 percent for people with no education and from 14 percent to 29.2 percent for people with a higher level education.

There are at least two possible explanations for this situation. The first stresses inadequate demand for labor. Educated Arab youth have traditionally been employed by the public sector. In fact, in many Arab countries youth with higher education were guaranteed a public job. As budgets got tighter and governments reduced (or even froze) hiring, the demand for qualified labor (or the supply of high-paying, secure jobs) declined sharply, especially since the private sector did not expand quickly enough. Thus many young people remain unemployed for extended periods of time waiting for a job opening in the public sector.

The second explanation stresses the mismatch between available skills and the skills demanded by a globalized labor market. It highlights two types of weaknesses in Arab education systems. The first concerns the quality of curricula. It is argued that education curricula in Arab countries rely too heavily on rote learning and do not help students acquire twenty-first-century skills, such as problem solving and working with a team, that are demanded by the labor market. The second concerns the delivery of the curricula. Results from international tests for mathematics and sciences indicate that too many Arab children are not learning, even though they attend school regularly.

Table 3-7 presents unemployment rates for Jordan disaggregated by education level and sex. It shows a similar relationship between education and unemployment as in Tunisia, except for the big spike in unemployment for men who have less than a secondary degree. Their unemployment rate is 60 percent compared with a 23 percent rate for those with higher education.

The relationship between education and unemployment for Jordanian women is particularly interesting. Female unemployment rises from 0.1 percent for illiterate women to nearly 70 percent for women with higher degrees (table 3-7). This could be explained by the fact that female labor force participation rates (which overall are only about 15 percent in Jordan) rise with education levels. Thus few illiterate women actually enter the labor market, hence their low unemployment

TABLE 3-7. Unemployment, by sex and educational level, Jordan, 2012

Percent

		Sex	
Education level	Total	Men	Women
Illiterate	0.9	1.3	0.1
Less than secondary	44.4	60.3	7.3
Secondary	8.2	10.0	3.8
Intermediate diploma	9.5	5.4	19.1
Bachelor and above	37.0	23.0	69.6

Source: Comolet (2014).

rate. On the other hand, many highly educated women enter the labor market, and their unemployment rate is three times as high as the unemployment rate for men with the same qualifications.

As shown in figure 3-4, most Arab youth who do find work end up having what is normally considered to be precarious employment, as self-employed, unpaid family workers and private informal wage earners. The public sector is still a significant employer in many Arab countries, but the formal private sector is still too small. For example, in Egypt, of the young men and women who do find jobs, only 38 percent find formal sector jobs—27 percent in the public sector and 11 percent in the formal private sector. The vast majority, 62 percent, end up working in the informal sector, often as unpaid family workers. For those who are paid, most have no labor contract, no job security, and no social benefits.

Table 3-8 shows that Arab youths' access to regular full-time employment is much lower than in all other regions of the world except for sub-Saharan Africa. Only 34 percent of young Arab males have full-time regular employment, compared with a world average of 47 percent. Similarly, only 31 percent of young Arab females have full-time employment, compared with a world average of 37 percent.

Table 3-8 also shows that the difference between Arab males and females in access to full-time regular employment is quite small (34 compared with 31 percent) and is smaller than what is observed in most of the other regions. Even in Europe the difference is much higher, with 60 percent of young males having regular full-time employment compared with only 49 percent of young females.

FIGURE 3-4. Work Status of Employed Individuals, Various Arab Countries, 2005–10

Percent

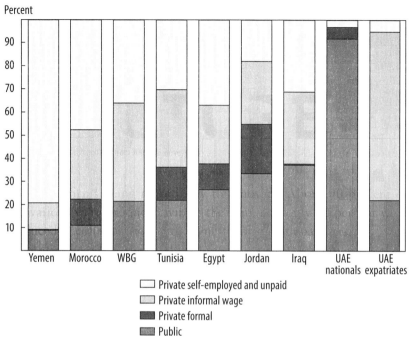

Private self-employed and unpaid
Private informal wage
Private formal
Public

Source: World Bank (2015).

How could the data in table 3-8 be reconciled with the huge gender gap observed in overall employment? The explanation lies in the big share of informal employment in overall employment and in Arab women's apparent belief that the informal sector is an unsafe environment for women. For example, in Egypt nearly all of the women working in the informal sector are in agriculture, working on the family farm with their husbands and children, and usually are not paid. Many Egyptian women explained that if they could not get a formal sector job, preferably in government, they prefer to "respect themselves" and stay at home.[12] This means that expanding formal employment will also have a positive impact on gender equality in most Arab countries.

Lack of economic opportunities naturally led to increased youth dissatisfaction and was one of the drivers of the revolutions. Gallup polled youth across the Arab world between February and April 2009

12. See World Bank (2012a).

TABLE 3-8. Share of Youth, Fifteen to Twenty-nine years, Working Full Time for an Employer
Percent

Region	Men	Women
Sub-Saharan Africa	20	16
Americas	56	40
Asia	48	41
Europe	60	49
Former Soviet Union countries	58	60
Arab world	34	31
World average	47	37

Source: Silatech Index Brief, 2013.

and showed that only 28 percent of Egyptian youth and 33 percent of Yemeni youth were satisfied with efforts to increase the supply of quality jobs in their countries. In Jordan and Tunisia, the figure is closer to 50 percent. In all of the Arab Spring countries, with the notable exception of Jordan, no more than 40 percent of youth felt that their countries' leadership was trying to maximize youth potential.

Young people suffered economic exclusion, and most blamed their countries' leadership for that state of affairs. This came on top of their feeling of social and political exclusion. Assaad and Barsoum (2007) studied the situation in Egypt and describe the constraints on self-expression faced by young men and women and the controls placed on student activities by the security apparatus. The result was that most young people refrained from any civic activities or volunteer work. They felt that their voices could not be heard. Many activist youth in Arab countries joined Islamist movements, which, according to Bayat (1998), provided them with an alternative moral and cultural community. Islamist organizations also provided youth with services, such as libraries and sports facilities, that the public sector was unable to deliver.

Inequalities Persist across Regions and between Rural and Urban Areas

The lower middle class and youth were not the only groups who felt excluded from the benefits of growth. Entire regions in the various

TABLE 3-9. Relative Importance of Agriculture, Arab Countries in Transition, 2013
Percent

Country	Agricultural value added as share of GDP	Agricultural employment as share of total employment	Rural population as share of total population
Egypt	15	29	57
Jordan	3	2	17
Morocco	17	39	41
Tunisia	9	16	34
Yemen	n.a.	25	67

Source: World Bank, World Development Indicators.

countries, mostly in rural areas, felt excluded as rural-urban and regional inequalities increased. This could explain why the Arab Spring started in Sidi Bouzid, a relatively underdeveloped and poor region in Tunisia.

Agriculture's role in most ACT economies and societies is much more important than is revealed by simply looking at its share in GDP. As shown in table 3-9, agriculture's contribution to GDP varies from a low of 3 percent in Jordan to 17 percent in Morocco. But this masks agriculture's important contribution to employment. As also shown in table 3-9, almost 40 percent of Morocco's labor force and 30 percent of the Egyptian labor force are employed in agriculture. Moreover, more than 40 percent of the Arab region's population (including 67 percent in Yemen and 57 percent in Egypt) lives in rural areas, and livelihoods are therefore either directly or indirectly affected by agriculture. Jordan is the outlier in this table, with a rural population that is only 17 percent of total population and with agricultural employment representing only 2 percent of total employment.

Agricultural yields in the ACTs are low by international standards. Low yields imply low labor productivity, low incomes, and high levels of rural poverty. World Development Indicators show that poverty in the ACTs is mostly a rural phenomenon. In Morocco, rural poverty is about three times higher than urban poverty, while in Egypt and Yemen it is twice as high.[13] In that sense the ACTs are not different from other developing (and even developed) countries, where large differences in

13. World Bank, World Development Indicators. Data from household surveys carried out at different times. The latest available year was used for each country.

living standards between urban and rural areas lead to migration out of rural areas and a process of urbanization. In the case of the ACTs the formal private sector has not been generating sufficient jobs. Hence the rural youth who migrated to cities ended up either unemployed or working in the informal sector. Thus they joined the ranks of the excluded and the dissatisfied.

In addition to the rural-urban differences, poverty in the ACTs also varies by region. Egypt and Tunisia provide good examples. In analyzing the incidence of poverty in Egypt it is useful to divide the country into four regions: metropolitan Egypt, which includes the large cities, especially Cairo and Alexandria; Lower Egypt, which includes the fertile delta region north of Cairo; Upper Egypt, which includes the Nile valley south of Cairo; and border regions, which include the desert areas along the border with Libya and in the Sinai. Each of these regions (except the metropolitan region) is divided into rural areas and urban centers.

Upper Egypt represents a special problem. It has about 50 percent of the country's population but 83 percent of the extremely poor and 67 percent of the poor. The problem in Upper Egypt is especially serious in the rural areas. Urban Upper Egypt has 11.6 percent of the extremely poor and 11.3 percent of the poor. On the other hand, rural Upper Egypt has 71.5 percent of the country's extremely poor and 55.8 percent of its poor.[14]

Table 3-10 presents the human opportunity index for the various Egyptian regions. This index was developed at the World Bank based on the idea that outcomes in terms of income and consumption are affected by the opportunities available to people, particularly to children. The concept behind the index is that people should be given an equal opportunity in life. The index can be aggregated into four groups describing access to different types of services: education (primary, secondary, and so on); adequate housing (water, sanitation, and so on); early childhood (prenatal and postnatal care, immunization, and so on); and nutrition (protection from wasting, stunting, and so on). Table 3-10 shows that Upper Egypt is the most lagging region in terms of education and adequate housing (particularly access to sanitation) and is the second most lagging in early childhood development and nutrition.

14. World Bank (2012b).

TABLE 3-10. Aggregate Human Opportunity Index, Egypt, by Region, 2009

Category	Metropolitan	Lower Egypt	Upper Egypt	Borders
Education	76	78	70	77
Housing	89	77	68	75
Early childhood	77	69	65	55
Nutrition	77	77	75	65

Source: World Bank (2012b).

People in Upper Egypt appear to have been excluded from the benefits of growth. This could explain, at least in part, the relative instability of that region and the spread of extremist ideologies among its youth.

In Tunisia, the western regions of the country are less developed than the eastern and coastal regions. Table 3-11 presents average annual consumption per capita across regions. It shows large inequalities with the level of per capita consumption in the richest region (Grand Tunis) more than double that of the poorest region (Midwest). In general, all the western regions (the interior) have lower per capita consumption than their eastern (coastal) counterparts. For example, average per capita consumption in the Northwest is only 76 percent of average per capita consumption in the Northeast. Moreover, per capita consumption has been growing at a slower rate in the West than in the East, implying increasing inequalities in spite of migration from West to East.

The lower average consumption levels in Tunisia are correlated with higher poverty. In the western regions, the poverty rates are indeed much higher than in the rest of the country: 32.3 percent, on average, in the Midwest and 25.9 percent in the Northwest, and again higher in the rural areas, about 50 percent higher than the national average and more than twice the poverty rate of big cities. Boughzala (2013) shows that all poverty rates, including those in the western regions, decreased significantly between 2000 and 2010, the decade before the revolution. However, the regional differences remained unchanged, which may explain the dissatisfaction felt by people in western Tunisia.

Sidi Bouzid, in midwestern Tunisia, is an example of a disadvantaged region in Tunisia and probably the rest of the Arab world. Agriculture is the main pillar of Sidi Bouzid's economy. Until the 1970s most of this agriculture was based on extensive cereal production and semi-nomadic sheep herding. Only a few small sedentary communities

TABLE 3-11. Per capita Consumption, Tunisia, by Region, 2010

Region	Per capita consumption (dinars; 2005 prices)		Annual growth rate (percent)	
	2000	2005	2010	2000–10
Grand Tunis	2,000	2,331	2,624	2.8
Northeast	1,320	1,547	1,718	2.7
Northwest	1,127	1,292	1,311	1.5
Mideast	1,707	1,902	2,189	2.5
Midwest	968	1,034	1,212	2.3
Southeast	1,126	1,574	1,787	4.7
Southwest	1,068	1,338	1,507	3.5
Tunisia	1,441	1,696	1,919	2.9

Source: Boughzala (2013).

had mastered vegetable growing. Within decades, a state-initiated process led to a deep transformation that turned the area's semi-nomadic people into peasants and farmers. The government adopted a three-pronged approach. First, tribal land was divided into private lots to provide the new private owners with an incentive to invest in agriculture. Second, the government built the first water systems based on ground water and deep aquifers and facilitated farmers' access to financial resources and to subsidized agricultural inputs, including seeds and fertilizers. Third, important public projects in infrastructure, roads, and electrical and safe-water networks were also completed to the benefit of the poor agricultural community.

Farmers responded quickly to the state's intervention. They invested in irrigation facilities even after the state, starting in the early 1990s, slowed down its interventions and stopped or reduced the subsidization of most of the inputs. Thus almost 90 percent of the irrigation investments—48,000 hectares of irrigated land—were the outcome of private investment. The total area has more than doubled since 1995; it increased from 223,000 hectares in 1995 to 488,000 hectares in 2012. This growth was mainly a private sector achievement. Thus by 2005 Sidi Bouzid had become a major producer of olive oil (9.5 percent of national production), almonds (23.8 percent), tomatoes (8.8 percent), and pomegranates (10 percent).

Incomes rose and living conditions improved in Sidi Bouzid, but many people, especially youth, did not benefit from this growth. Investors from outside the region, mainly from Sfax, developed large modern farms concentrated in the most fertile part of Sidi Bouzid. Small local farmers felt excluded.

Young people in Sidi Bouzid benefited from secondary and tertiary education. They expected this would be the key to better employment, but for a large number of them this did not happen. Few employment opportunities were available. In 2010 the average unemployment rate for university graduates in Sidi Bouzid was around 40 percent. It was even higher for young women, many of whom simply exited the labor market. The only jobs available were for seasonal, low-paid farm laborers, jobs that do not interest educated youth. Young people were also unable to start farming businesses because they lacked the financial resources and had no access to land. Sidi Bouzid's youth were forced to join a long waiting list for a government job.

It All Started in Sidi Bouzid

The educated youth of Sidi Bouzid were frustrated and ready to express their anger by all available means. Their anger peaked on December 17, 2010, when police confiscated the cart and scales of a twenty-six-year-old informal vegetable seller, Mohamed Bouazizi. When he tried to argue with them because he needed the cart and the scale to support his mother and six siblings, a policeman slapped him in the face. He went to complain to the municipality and the governorate but was turned away. Humiliated, angry, and frustrated, he burnt himself in front of the governorate headquarters. This sparked a rebellion in Sidi Bouzid and ignited a massive uprising in Tunisia that quickly spread to the rest of the Arab world. Mohamed Bouazizi died of his burns on January 4, 2011.

Bouazizi's action and consequent revolutions in Tunisia and elsewhere obviously had a political and governance dimension. This was not the first time that the police harassed Bouazizi: they had done that occasionally to extort payments from him. But this time he apparently refused, or maybe he did not have enough to pay them off. The authorities had no respect for human rights or citizens' dignity. The policeman slapped him. Bouazizi felt that he did not have any voice. He tried complaining to the municipality and to the governorate but he was ignored. Government officials, particularly the police, were not accountable for their actions. They could confiscate Bouazizi's property and even slap him without being questioned about their actions.

But didn't Bouazizi's action and the consequent revolution also have an economic and social dimension? Would that incident have occurred if Bouazizi had had a regular full-time job? Would it have occurred if he had been the owner of an officially sanctioned small business rather than an informal enterprise operating in the shadows of legality and thus vulnerable to police extortion? Would this incident have occurred if his mother or one of his sisters had a job so that the weight of supporting the entire family did not fall on his shoulders alone?

It seems to me that economic issues were central to the Arab Spring. This also means that social and political stability in most Arab countries will remain elusive until those socioeconomic issues are resolved. Returning to past policies, generating growth and waiting for it to trickle down to the middle class and the poor, is not good enough. The Arab world needs to consider a change in economic policies, focusing on inclusive growth—that is, growth that expands the middle class, enhances social justice, and increases opportunities for all citizens.

4

Institutional Reforms for Better Implementation

The World Bank has stated that "weak governance has led to weak growth in MENA [the Middle East and North Africa]. . . . Indeed, simulations find that if MENA had matched the average quality of administration in the public sector for a group of well-performing Southeast Asian countries (Indonesia, Malaysia, the Philippines, Singapore and Thailand), its growth rates would have been higher by about one percentage point a year."[1] Economic institutions and governance arrangements affect growth in many different ways, but excellent economic plans, programs, and projects are not of much use if they are not implemented. Weak institutions and inadequate governance arrangements in Arab countries lead to the adoption of plans and policies that while they may be technically sound, do not necessarily reflect the needs of different stakeholders. Those institutional and governance weaknesses imply that the plans, programs, and projects are often not implemented.

Governance is a complex concept, and I present different definitions in the following section. Throughout this book I focus on just two pillars of good governance: inclusiveness and accountability. Good governance requires institutions that are both inclusive and accountable. I focus on those two components of good governance because they have been identified by several authors as areas where Arab countries are particularly weak and lag behind other nations of similar per capita

---

1. World Bank (2003, pp. 8–9).

income and level of development.[2] Such lack of inclusiveness and weak accountability affect implementation of projects and programs.[3]

Governance, Institutions, and Economic Growth

According to Keefer (2004, p. 3), "Governance is the extent to which the institutions and processes of government give government decision makers an incentive to be responsive to citizens." That is, good governance is about putting in place institutions and processes that ensure that economic decisions reflect the citizens' will. This view of what is good governance seems to be also the one adopted by the United Nations Development Program (UNDP). Its website states that "more countries than ever before are working to build democratic governance. Their challenge is to develop institutions and processes that are more responsive to the needs of ordinary citizens, including the poor, and that promote development."[4] The agency's definition of good governance goes beyond that presented by Keefer, because it specifically mentions democratic governance, and it specifies that institutions need to be responsive to ordinary citizens, including the poor.

The World Bank's Worldwide Governance Indicators computes systematic measures of governance. It looks at six groups of governance indicators: voice and accountability, political stability, government effectiveness, control of corruption, regulatory quality, and rule of law.[5] This reflects the breadth of the concept of governance and the general view that a system of good governance should give more voice to citizens, hold governments accountable, lead to more effective bureaucracies, lower corruption, improve the regulatory framework, and respect the rule of law.

---

2. For example, the United Nations Development Program (2002).

3. This chapter is based on research carried out by a team of JICA and Brookings scholars, and particularly Sakamoto (2013), Matsunaga and Ragheb (2015), and Tanaka and Yoshikawa (2013). The work of those authors has focused on Egypt and Iraq, and hence most of the examples presented here are from those two countries. However, lessons drawn from this work are relevant across the Arab world.

4. See United Nations Development Program, "Democratic Governance" (www.undp.org/content/undp/en/home/ourwork/democraticgovernance/overview.html).

5. See Kaufmann, Kraay, and Mastruzi (2008).

In its 2003 report on governance in the MENA region, the World Bank stresses the importance of inclusiveness and accountability. It defines an inclusive institution as one that guarantees certain basic rights to all citizens. This means that all citizens have the right to participate in decisionmaking processes on an equal basis. It also means that government must treat all citizens equally. An accountable institution is defined as one in which leaders are answerable to the people for their decisions. Accountability requires transparency, for people need to know how the government is functioning to hold it accountable. It also needs contestability, for people should be able to choose among different entities on the basis of how well they perform. It also implies the existence of recourse mechanisms, for it is hard to achieve full accountability by simply putting in place internal accountability mechanisms within the public administration, especially in countries where the executive is able to overpower other branches of government. That is why accountability usually requires inclusiveness so that citizens have voice and can express their views on government performance.

The development literature has focused mostly on the relation between governance and growth.[6] Most studies show a positive correlation between different governance indicators, particularly those relating to the security of property rights and government effectiveness and to growth. However, the direction of causality is not always clear. Good governance facilitates growth, but it is also true that growing countries with higher incomes demand better governance. That is, governance is also endogenous to growth. The ideal is to achieve a virtuous circle where governance reforms support growth, which, in turn, leads to better governance and even faster growth.

Acemoglu and Robinson (2012) argue that the main (or even only) explanation for different economic outcomes among countries is different institutions. Economic institutions are important in determining economic outcomes. Inclusive institutions lead to the creation of inclusive markets that support growth and equality of opportunity. On the other hand, extractive institutions stifle entrepreneurship and creativity and thus lead to low growth and high inequality. According to Acemoglu and Robinson, it is political institutions that determine what kind of economic institutions develop in a country. Hence a country's

6. For example, see Calderon and Chong (2000); Easterly and Levine (2002).

economic development is driven by its politics. Relatively open political systems that provide voice for their citizens and allow them to hold governments accountable naturally lead to inclusive economic institutions. In their discussion of Egypt, Acemoglu and Robinson argue that "Egypt is poor precisely because it has been ruled by a narrow elite that has organized society for their own benefit at the expense of the vast mass of the people. Political power has been narrowly concentrated, and was used to create great wealth for those who possess it."[7]

Sakamoto (2013) argues that lack of transparency and low accountability in Arab countries has led to greater corruption and the emergence of "a soft state."[8] A sense of alienation and exclusion, especially among youth, contributed to popular dissatisfaction, which continues even after the revolutions. That is why, he argues, there is a need to improve participation in policymaking and economic planning in the Arab world. The experiences of Japan, Malaysia, and Indonesia indicate the importance of achieving a national consensus on an economic vision for the future and the policies and programs needed to achieve it. Successful East Asian countries have put in place consultative processes (in different government departments, the private sector, and civil society) to agree on national development plans and monitor their execution.

Arab countries are aware of this lacuna, and some of them are starting to take steps to improve inclusion and accountability. For example, articles 12–15 of the new Moroccan constitution set out inclusive participation in government decision making as a fundamental principle. Morocco asked for World Bank support to put in place a legal and regulatory framework for access to information to enhance transparency. Morocco is also introducing reforms to extend the scope of public consultations and enable citizens to petition the government and make legislative proposals.[9] Similarly, Egypt has been receiving support from the Japan International Cooperation Agency (JICA) to introduce inclusive planning.

Enhancing the planning function is essential to improving the allocation of public investment and to raising its efficiency. Inclusive planning

---

7. See Acemoglu and Robinson (2012), preface.
8. Sakamoto (2013, p. 7).
9. See World Bank (2013b).

TABLE 4-1. Gross Fixed Capital Formation as Share of GDP, Various Countries, 1980–2013
Percent

Country	1980	1990	2000	2010	2013
Brazil	23	20	18	20	18
China	35	36	35	48	49
India	18	25	24	37	30
Egypt	28	29	20	19	14
Jordan	37	31	22	24	28
Morocco	24	25	26	35	n.a.
Tunisia	29	27	26	24	n.a.
Yemen	n.a.	12	19	n.a.	n.a.

Source: World Development Indicators.

could also increase ownership of the investment program by different stakeholders. Widespread buy-in helps improve implementation rates and thus could lead to an increase in overall investment levels.

Low Investment Rates in the Arab Countries in Transition

Economic growth usually requires the accumulation of physical capital, whether as infrastructure or as new buildings, factories, machinery, and equipment. Table 4-1 shows the evolution of the ratio of investment to GDP in the Arab countries in transition (ACTs) and three comparator countries. Two points are worth noting. First, in 2013 investment rates in the ACTs were comparable to those of Brazil but much lower than those of India, which invests about a third of GDP, and especially China, which invests nearly half of GDP. Second, on average, ACT investment rates seem to be stagnating or declining (with the notable exception of Morocco), while investment rates in China and India (but not Brazil) have been increasing.

To catch up with the emerging economies, the ACTs will probably need to raise their investment rates. This would require an increase in both public and private investment. Public investment that improves the quality of infrastructure would encourage greater private sector investment, through a crowding-in effect.

Figures 4-1 and 4-2 show the evolution of public and private investment in Jordan and Egypt over the past thirty years. They tell a similar

FIGURE 4-1. Public and Private Investment as Share of GDP, Jordan, 1976–2012

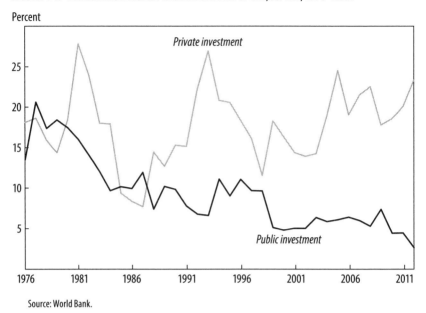

Source: World Bank.

FIGURE 4-2. Public and Private Investment as Share of GDP, Egypt, 1982–2012

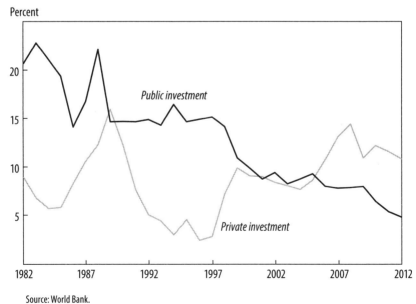

Source: World Bank.

story. Private investment has stagnated at around 20 percent of GDP in Jordan and 10 percent of GDP in Egypt, while public investment has declined dramatically from about 20 percent of GDP in both countries to less than 5 percent. This is very different from the experience of countries like India and China, where both private and public investment increased.

The quality of institutions affects private as well as public investment. Noninclusive institutions have a negative impact on the business environment and therefore lead to a reduction in private investment. Experience in some ACTs indicates that simply reforming the rules on the books may not have an impact, because the reforms may be poorly implemented or not implemented at all.[10] It is important that the institutions responsible for implementing the regulatory framework affecting the private sector be reformed to become more inclusive (so that the private sector has a say in how regulations are implemented) and accountable (so that the institution is judged on its results and the quality of service it provides).

Not all public investment is good for growth. In a weak institutional framework poorly designed or implemented public investment could be counterproductive, introducing distortions and inefficiencies in the economy and providing opportunities for corruption. Moreover, if the macroeconomic framework is weak, increasing public investment could lead to more serious fiscal imbalances and debt problems.

Inclusive Planning in Egypt and East Asia

Sakamoto (2013) studied the planning process in Egypt and compared it with that of East Asia.[11] He found that during the period 1982–2000, Egypt had fourteen plans, three visions, seven strategies, and three programs, among others. In total there were forty-one schemes individually drafted by ministries and relevant organizations with support from international donors. They do not seem to have been related or systematically linked to one another. The national five-year plan was supposed to be the guiding document for economic policy.

10. For an example from Egypt, see Ghanem (2013).
11. This section draws on the work of Sakamoto (2013).

Egypt had six national five-year plans between 1982 and 2011. Budget allocations were determined before drafting the economic goals and strategies. The first planning step was the production of the investment budget allocation sheet, which was put together by the Ministry of Planning, based on the investment budget request prepared by each line ministry. The contents of the five-year development plan were then drafted by the Ministry of Planning based on the budget allocation sheet. This system was simple, with drafting being fully completed inside the ministry without official outside contacts. On the other hand, the system led to the exclusion of major stakeholders, such as the private sector, civil society organizations, labor unions, and the media.

This does not mean that there was no interaction between government and the private sector. But communication and cooperation occurred without an institutional dialogue mechanism. This led to numerous collusive relationships and hence the risk of corruption. Some privileged private companies benefited, while others were left in the lurch. Sakamoto (2013) describes this situation as the emergence of the soft state.

None of the plans had a strategy for implementation. Since the five-year plans in Egypt were drafted inside one department of the Ministry of Planning without building consensus among major stakeholders, including line ministries, which were the real implementers, the national plan was viewed as a concept paper that did not call for execution. Plans, visions, and strategies were well prepared but never implemented. To deal with those problems, Handoussa (2010) proposed a mechanism, based on uniform and fair rules, for including academics and civil society organizations in the planning process. However, those proposals have so far not been implemented.

The situation in many other Arab countries is similar to that of Egypt. Plans have been developed that are technically sound but are not necessarily implemented, and the public investments that are included in those plans are not fully realized.

But is planning really needed in today's market economies? Experience from successful East Asian countries indicates that the answer is yes but that planning today plays a different role from the one that it played in the 1950s and 1960s. In the twenty-first century, economic planning plays two roles. First, it introduces a mechanism for a societal dialogue on economic issues; and second, it develops consensus on a medium- to long-term vision for economic growth. That is, the plan should be the result of an inclusive process and should present a guiding vision for economic development. Former Indonesian president Susilo Bambang Yudhoyono, in his presentation of the 2011 economic plan, stated that "it is impossible to achieve our long-term economic goals without the master plan. We also can't rely wholly on market mechanisms. The government's role, as a 'visible hand,' is important."[12]

Successful East Asian economies were the first group of countries to develop strategies for inclusive growth. To achieve this, they put in place systems of inclusive planning. Arab countries could benefit from the experiences of countries like Japan, Malaysia, and Indonesia.

Since the end of World War II, Japan has developed fourteen economic plans as follows: the first plan targeted reconstruction and independence, the second and third plans aimed for high economic growth, the fourth, fifth, and sixth tried to balance economic growth with social development, and the seventh to fourteenth strived for stable growth.

Japan's Economic Council was created to build national consensus on economic issues and to draft the five-year plans. It was established in 1952, under the Ministry of Economy, Trade, and Industry, as the advisory body for the prime minister. It includes government officials, academics, private sector representatives, labor unions, the media, consumer representatives, and civil society. Thus it plays a key role in coordinating interests and resolving conflicts among stakeholders. Line ministries (the implementers) participate actively in the planning process. Thus they own the outcome and are bound by the results, which is one of the reasons why all the Japanese plans were fully implemented ahead of the original schedule.

An effective system for planning, monitoring, and evaluation contributed to Malaysia's socioeconomic success.[13] Malaysia's Economic Planning Unit, which functions as a superministry, is attached to the prime minister's office. It takes the leading role in formulating the coordination plans with the National Budget Office. It is also in charge of drafting the five-year plans as well as their mid-term reviews. The Implementation Coordination Unit, also under the prime minister's office, is responsible for supervising plan implementation, working

12. Quoted in Sakamoto (2013, p. 12).
13. See United Nations (2001).

with the line ministries. By placing the Economic Planning Unit and the Implementation Coordination Unit under the authority of the prime minister's office, the government created a strong administrative body that enhanced the efficiency of the planning process and ensured effective implementation.

The implementation function is further strengthened by the inclusion of various stakeholders and the institutionalization of public-private dialogues, at regional as well as federal levels. Thus the Malaysian system is comparable to the Japanese Economic Council, with a strong focus on plan implementation. While impact evaluation at the project level was undertaken by each of the ministries, it was the Implementation Coordination Unit that conducted the impact evaluation at the macro level. The agency also developed various monitoring systems, which involved the periodic collection and analysis of physical and financial data.

Inspired by the Japanese and Malaysian experiences, Indonesia changed its economic decision, after the fall of the Suharto regime, from a top-down planning process to a bottom-up approach. The Development Planning Committee was strengthened in 2004 and expanded to include citizen representatives. Thus coordination between stakeholders became institutionalized, allowing the voices of citizens to be reflected in policies and helping build consensus around economic policies. Moreover, starting in 2009, national dialogues with the thirty-two governors and chief executive officers of the chambers of commerce were organized once every several months to build consensus and ownership of the major implementers (local government and the private sector) of the economic plan.

From Plan to Implementation in Cairo's Urban Transport

Cairo is one of the most congested cities in the world. The World Bank estimates the cost, mostly because of fuel and time lost in traffic, at about 4 percent of GDP.[14] A 2002 study carried out jointly by the Egyptian government and JICA concluded that if no major reforms and new

14. See World Bank (2014a). This section relies on the work of Matsunaga and Ragheb (2015).

investments were implemented, by 2022 the average trip speed would decline from 19 kilometers an hour to 11.6 kilometers an hour and the average home-to-work trip time by car would increase from 37 minutes to 100 minutes. Recent updates of the study by the Egyptian Ministry of Transport yield worse results. Trip speed is expected to drastically worsen to reach 5 kilometers an hour and trip time to reach 240 minutes, or four hours, by 2022 if nothing is done to improve the situation. That is, this study implies that, under a business-as-usual scenario, in less than ten years the average Cairo resident will spend at least as much time in traffic as at work.

Faced with this disastrous situation the Ministry of Transport formulated the Transport Master Plan in 2002 and carried out feasibility studies—the Cairo Regional Area Transportation Study (CREATS)—for selected priority projects in 2003.[15] The ministry also tried to formulate the plan in an inclusive way. Key stakeholders were invited to participate at the planning stage. These included the Ministry of Transport, the Egypt National Institute of Transport, the National Authority for Tunnels, the Egyptian National Railways Authority, the General Authority for Roads Bridges and Land Transport, and Cairo and Giza governorates as well as private sector and civil society representatives. The planning process was supported by JICA and appears to have been carried out efficiently and achieved good results.

Yet the plan was not implemented, and Cairo's traffic situation continues to deteriorate. The plan recommended fifty-nine actions, including new investments and policy reforms. About thirteen years later, only four of those fifty-nine actions had been initiated. Matsunaga and Ragheb (2015) identify five possible reasons for the failure to implement: lack of proper authorization for the plan, weak coordination among the concerned agencies and lack of a focal point, insufficient institutional capacity, budget limitations and lack of private sector participation, and inability to reduce fuel subsidies.

In Egypt, sector or regional master plans and strategies are approved by the concerned minister. They do not necessarily receive cabinet or parliamentary approval. Ministers change often in Egypt. Hence the minister who approved a plan or strategy is often not around when

---

15. See Arab Republic of Egypt and Japan International Cooperation Agency (2002).

implementation is expected to start. New ministers are often not committed to their predecessors' plans and strategies and do not push for implementation. The transport plan was approved by a so-called higher committee chaired by the minister of transport. But the minister and many members of the committee were replaced after the plan's approval, and the committee itself stopped meeting, even though legally it still exists. Thus the legal status of the transport master plan is unclear, and the Ministry of Transport does not feel obliged to implement it. In other words, no one in government seems to be held accountable for dealing with Cairo's traffic problems.

Coordinating the various stakeholders is another big problem. The Ministry of Transport supervises twelve entities: six service authorities and six economic authorities, each of which is in charge of a specific transport subsector. The coordination problem is not only in vertical coordination within the Ministry of Transport and its affiliated entities or between central and local levels but also in horizontal coordination and linkage among concerned ministries and agencies beyond the realm of the Ministry of Transport. In the case of the urban transportation, other ministries and agencies such as the Ministry of Housing, the Ministry of Interior, and Cairo and Giza governorates are key stakeholders. In 2013 a regulatory agency for urban transport was created, partly to act as a focal agency that can mediate among all stakeholders and help improve coordination. However, it is still not functioning and has only one professional staff working there.

Other countries are facing similar coordination problems. The situation in Thailand is even more difficult than in Egypt. More than thirty institutions are involved in urban transport development in Thailand, but the country has somehow managed to develop the infrastructure since the early 1990s. Manila was quite the same until it formed the Strategic Metropolitan Transport Planning in 1995 (Mandri-Perrott 2010). Jakarta is trying to manage the adverse impacts of institutional fragmentation by establishing a metropolitan transportation authority, known as the Jabodetabek Transportation Authority, at the central government level with participation of more than fifteen relevant entities to facilitate the implementation process through coordination of activities while avoiding any overlap. Many other countries (for example, India, Singapore, and China) have established focal or lead institutions for managing urban transport development. Hence Egypt's new Agency for Urban Transport could benefit from those countries' experiences.

Institutional capacity is a major constraint on implementation. Leadership is one of the factors that affect the capacity of any organization. In the case of the Ministry of Transport, frequent changes of ministers (there have been seven ministers over the past three years) have negatively impacted continuity. The Ministry of Transport is a hierarchical top-down organization, with a relatively weak back office. Therefore, ministerial changes typically lead to changes in direction and strategy.

The lack of a technical back office with qualified staff is another important constraint. Although the ministry, like the rest of the Egyptian civil service, has a huge number of administrative staff, it has few technical specialists. An exacerbating factor is that instead of focusing on its key strategic and policymaking role, the ministry is often excessively involved in operational issues, spreading itself too thin.

It is useful to compare Cairo's experience with that of New Delhi. Cairo was one of the first cities in the developing world to introduce a metro system, in 1987. The system has seen little extension, and after twenty-five years it consists of three lines with a total of 69 kilometers. The metro system in Delhi started to operate in 2002, fifteen years later, but it already has six lines for a total of 190 kilometers. Differences in institutional capacity could explain the different outcomes. In Cairo, the weak capacity of the National Authority for Tunnels may be behind the weak performance. In New Delhi, an executing agency, Delhi Metro Rail Corporation Limited, was established in 1995 and was a driving force in implementing the development of Delhi Metro as scheduled. Construction work on the New Delhi metro has not suffered from the long delays experienced in Cairo.

Could the difference in performance between the Cairo and New Delhi metro systems be explained by factors other than institutional capacity (for example, availability of financing)? It does not seem so. The Japan International Cooperation Agency has funded both the Delhi Metro and the Cairo Metro No. 4 under its soft-loan scheme. Construction of the Delhi metro did not face any delays, whereas the Cairo Metro No. 4 is facing a two-year delay and a new extension of Cairo Metro No. 3 is six years late.

Ministry of Transport staff complain that tight budgets are the most important reason for the weak implementation. It is true that the urban transport system needs huge investments and that resources are scarce. One way of dealing with tight budgets is to improve cost recovery. Very little was done in this area. Currently, the price of a metro ticket is about US$0.14, far below what is needed to recover the cost of investment.

Another way of dealing with tight budgets is to attract private sector participation, but Egypt has not been successful in this regard. This is very different from the experience of Asian countries, who were able to mobilize large amounts of private capital. In Manila, a public-private partnership was used to develop an expressway and the city's Light Rail Transit. Metro Manila Skyway was developed by a joint venture, and the Southern Tagalog Arterial Road is a build-own-transfer project. In Bangkok, the Second Stage Expressway System was built using a build-transfer-operate scheme. Two lines of the elevated railway system and one line of the subway were built by public-private partnerships.

It must be noted, however, that these Asian experiences were not without their own problems. While they succeeded in attracting private investment to build the urban transport infrastructure based on private participation, several projects faced financial sustainability challenges. In the Philippines, government kept fares very low and had to make large subsidy payments to the private operator to ensure a minimum return on his investment. Similarly, in Bangkok, low tolls on the expressway reduced the profitability of the foreign investor, who ultimately sold his shares to a local company.

The lesson from the Asian experience is that it is possible to mobilize large amounts of private investment for the transport sector. However, the long-term sustainability of those investments depends on the adoption of pricing policies that reflect the cost of the service and ensure an adequate return on investment.

In addition to investments to expand the transport system, most countries adopt measures to restrict demand and reduce congestion. For example, to restrict car use and encourage reliance on public transport, Jakarta initiated the so-called three-in-one scheme, requiring that vehicles entering the city carry at least three passengers during peak hours. Manila had introduced a color coding program in 1996 that does not allow cars with certain number plates to drive in the city within certain hours on weekdays. Manila also introduced truck bans and bus priority lanes to reduce traffic congestion. Bangkok's Intelligent Traffic Information System provides drivers with traffic information in order to avoid congested areas.

Proper pricing, through car licensing fees, parking fees, toll prices, and fuel prices, is probably the most effective demand management measure. By increasing the cost of vehicle operation, this measure promotes greater use of public transportation and hence less traffic congestion. In Egypt, fuel prices are heavily subsidized, which encourages greater car use, congestion, and pollution. The government started reducing fuel subsidies in July 2014. As subsidies are reduced further and fuel prices increase to reach world levels, more people will start using public transportation instead of private cars, which should lead to less congestion and less air pollution.

Involvement of Donors in Iraq

Implementation is a serious problem in Iraq, an example of a fragile country that is reconstructing in a context of political instability and weak governance.[16] According to the World Bank's Worldwide Governance Indicators, Iraq is ranked twentieth from the bottom, after Liberia and the Republic of the Congo, in government effectiveness and fifth, after Sudan and Afghanistan, in political stability.[17] In addition, owing to decades of economic sanctions, Iraq's government officials have limited knowledge and experience in international commercial activities, further discouraging foreign businesses. Even official donors avoid implementing large-scale projects.

To address these difficulties, JICA and the Iraqi government agreed to introduce a unique monitoring platform composed of three pillars: increased interaction, a multilayer structure, and the presence of the UNDP. A first priority was to build the capacity of Iraqi staff, who had little experience implementing donor-financed projects. Project entities set up a project management team for each project, and the Iraqi

16. This section relies on the work of Tanaka and Yoshikawa (2013).
17. Worldwide Governance Indicators, 2011 data.

government decided to limit staff rotations so as to encourage capacity development and knowledge sharing. Each team has to submit a monthly project progress report. The Japan International Cooperation Agency reviews the report and provides feedback. The progress report and feedback cover important aspects of project management and contribute to establishing the project management framework. Regular and structured interaction between the relatively inexperienced Iraqi staff and their JICA counterparts is designed to build capacity and help Iraqi staff identify the main constraints on project implantation and develop ways of resolving them.

Second, a multilayered monitoring system was introduced, and a committee including representatives from high-level oversight agencies such as the Prime Minister's Advisory Commission, the Ministry of Finance, and the Ministry of Planning was established to periodically oversee the various projects. Quarterly monitoring meetings that included all the relevant actors were introduced. In those meetings, project entities discuss best practices and common problems, while JICA and the high-level oversight agencies evaluate project entities based on measureable factors of their performance. They praise project management teams that had good performance records and encourage those that have bad performance records to improve.

Third, JICA and the Iraqi government agreed to partner with the UNDP to provide additional support to project implementation. The UNDP staff had easier access to projects in areas affected by strife than JICA officials and thus were better able to capture actual implementation problems through direct access rather than via emails or phone calls. Based on the findings, they provide analyses and evaluations in monthly reports and quarterly monitoring meetings. In addition, the presence of the UNDP alleviated an unequal relationship between donor and recipient. Such imbalanced relationships or feelings between donors and recipients are often observed in implementation of aid projects. But being a recognized international organization, the UNDP's assessments are considered to be an independent third-party's opinion, which contributes not only to maintaining a well-balanced relationship among stakeholders but also to improving monitoring effectiveness.

This system has led to an improvement in the implementation efficiency of JICA's projects in Iraq. For example, during the course of implementation, the average lapse of JICA's review of documents on each procurement process has become shorter, suggesting that the quality of the documents prepared by the government has improved and that aid projects will be completed sooner.[18]

Tanaka and Yoshikawa (2013) compare the efficiency of JICA projects across different countries, using the time taken to complete the project as a proxy for efficiency. They conclude that the Iraqi government manages JICA projects more effectively than the average country. They also compare the efficiency of JICA projects in Iraq with those of the World Bank. They conclude that efficiency rates improve over time for both JICA projects and World Bank projects. However, the efficiency rate for JICA projects exceeds that for World Bank projects over time, while the efficiency rate for the World Bank's projects is better at the beginning. Thus JICA's projects in Iraq could be considered an example of successful implementation. But what are the causal factors behind this success?

Three mechanisms were introduced in Iraq by JICA: increased interaction (a knowledge-sharing mechanism), a multilayer structure (a social recognition mechanism), and the presence of the UNDP (a mediation mechanism). The three mechanisms were introduced at the same time. Hence it is difficult to disentangle them and measure the impact of each mechanism separately.

Increased interactions with Iraqi officials were aimed at knowledge sharing and capacity building. Tanaka and Yoshikawa (2013) focus on two aspects of interactions: quality and quantity. Increased interactions and knowledge sharing should in principle enhance the implementation capacity of the Iraqi teams. But what is more important, the quantity of interactions or their quality? To reduce misunderstanding and help Iraqi officials accumulate relevant knowledge, JICA increased

18. In each step of procurement, JICA requires project entities to submit procurement documents and reviews the documents against JICA's procurement guidelines, which indicates basic guidance in international bid procedure. Prequalification documents' average lapse and bidding documents' average lapse mean the number of days taken by JICA for review of prequalification documents and bid documents, respectively. In case of prequalification result and bidding result, JICA reviews the evaluation process and the result described in the evaluation documents.

communications with them at all levels. At the same time it improved the content of monitoring and gave the officials more detailed feedback.

Social recognition was also used to improve performance. The UNDP and JICA published a project-entity ranking based on their performance every year. Using the ranking, Iraqi authorities praised project entities that performed well and criticized those that failed to achieve their targets. Thus project teams that received good evaluations were motivated to work efficiently to maintain their record, and teams that received bad evaluations tried to improve to avoid social punishment and become recognized as good achievers.

The UNDP partnered with JICA to help with capacity development and to provide a mediation mechanism between donor and recipient institutions. According to Tanaka and Yoshikawa (2013), the UNDP's participation had two positive impacts. First, UNDP officials' ability to move easily across the country while introducing UNDP-facilitated project management allowed face-to-face interactions that resulted in more efficient project management. Second, since Iraqi officials consider the UNDP a neutral third party, the Iraqi officials seemed to have more frank conversations with UNDP officials, leading to early detection of problems and more efficient project management.

Tanaka and Yoshikawa (2013) carried out econometric analyses to see how the different mechanisms affected implementation capacity. This analysis indicates that project teams that received more feedback from JICA or the UNDP tended to improve their work effectiveness over time, but that the number of interactions or communications may not be as important an indicator as the quality of interactions—that is, the quality of interaction is more important than its quantity. The analysis also shows that the more negative evaluations a project team received in the previous year, the more likely its work effectiveness was to increase. This implies that the social recognition mechanism works better for those who receive negative evaluations than for those who receive positive evaluations.

Hence it would appear that donor agencies have a role to play in enhancing implementation capacity, even under the difficult situation of a fragile state facing civil conflict and widespread unrest. Mechanisms for knowledge sharing and for social recognition could be powerful tools for enhancing institutional capacity and improving the efficiency of project implementation.

Suggestions for Improvement

The analysis presented here indicates that successful implementation requires inclusive planning to help build support for the economic program, the development of implementation strategies while formulating plans and strategies, and a process for the legitimization of plans. In addition, there is a need to reform and strengthen economic institutions and hold them accountable for implementation and to ensure that sufficient resources are mobilized to cover implementation and finally strengthen monitoring and evaluation systems.

The Egyptian case study demonstrates that often, though a great deal of resources and energy are exerted in the planning phase, after the formulation of a plan less attention and fewer resources are directed toward implementation. But is there value to a plan that is not implemented? It may have some political value. Announcing good intentions could attract some support, at least initially, until citizens realize that nothing has really changed on the ground. It could also have some bureaucratic value. Writing and rewriting plans and strategies is one way for civil servants to justify their jobs and salaries. But it certainly has no economic value. A plan to build a new metro line would not reduce traffic congestion. It is the actual building of the new metro line that reduces congestion.

Though a great deal of effort is often exerted, planning in the ACTs could still be improved. The experience of East Asia underlines the importance of involving all stakeholders. Presumably listening to the voices of all concerned citizens would help improve the quality of the plan by making sure that it responds to real needs. Moreover, buy-in at the planning stage by all those involved in implementation could help improve execution, as all stakeholders would cooperate to ensure that the plan they developed together is actually implemented and actually bears fruit. It is important to ensure ownership of the plan by those who are supposed to implement it.

Plans and strategies must be complemented with implementation plans that clarify in detail how to execute the plan with identified actions, timelines, and concerned stakeholders. These drivers can be consolidated into an execution or implementation plan. Executing agencies often complain that they have difficulty figuring out how to realize the strategies, since the strategies tend to describe overall direction and broad visions and projects with little or no guidance on how they could be achieved.

Plans and strategies need to be seen as legitimate by various stakeholders if they are to be effectively implemented. Legitimization is important for any policy action since it will provide priority, momentum, and support for implementation, especially when there is a strain on the budget resources. If legitimacy is not appropriately secured, the stakeholders will not recognize the need to comply with the plan and to work on achieving it.

How can a plan be legitimized? In some cases legitimacy is conferred on a plan by the top political leadership, the president or the prime minister. The project to expand the Suez Canal in Egypt provides an example, as it was identified as a priority by the president, who obtained support of the cabinet for the project. Parliaments can also legitimize economic plans, for example by voting on five-year plans as well as on the budgets to implement them. Plans and strategies that are simply approved by the sector or line ministry are rarely fully implemented.

A plan could also be seen as legitimate because it attracts a high level of public support. In addition to acquiring authorization and legitimization from the government, the support of final beneficiaries is needed to ensure success. In other words, getting buy-in from the public is another key factor for the success of implementation.

Constituency building to obtain public support for economic plans is a weak area in nearly all Arab countries, as they tend to rely on top-down legitimization processes. Plans or policy reforms need to be marketed and promoted, and they need to acquire public support to be implemented successfully. The wider public should be well informed about the benefits and demerits from the implementation of a plan or public reform since there will inevitably be both winners and losers once some kind of change takes place. The general public needs to understand why policy reforms are being implemented and how the majority of the population will benefit from them. Communication is essential to building trust and credibility for the government and to keep citizens involved, increase their sense of ownership, and reduce information asymmetries among stakeholders involved. It is easier to persuade people to accept the new strategies when they feel they are part of the decision and implementation process.

Reforms of public sector management and institutions are often needed to solve implementation problems. A comprehensive civil service reform is usually politically difficult and time consuming. However, some changes, those that do not require use of a great deal of political capital, can be introduced to improve the public sector's implementation capacity. Improving coordination among public sector institutions is one such change. This would include vertical coordination to improve the line of command inside a ministry, between a ministry and subordinated executing agencies, and between upstream core economic ministries such as the Ministry of Finance or the Ministry of Planning and downstream bodies, including sector ministries and nonexecutive state institutions. It would also include horizontal coordination across different ministries and departments.

Some countries (for example, Malaysia) have created a focal organizational body to improve horizontal coordination. An organization that includes various government and nongovernment representatives such as a national economic council might become a good mechanism for promoting an economic reform program. Following the Japanese example, such a council can become an authorizing body for plans and strategies, and it can strengthen coordination among various stakeholders to enhance implementation efficiency.

What should be the role and functions of central economic agencies like the ministries of planning and finance and the central bank, and how could they improve coordination? Countries' institutional designs for central economic agencies are diverse, reflecting different political, economic, and social contexts. This introduces a subset of questions that need to be addressed: What would be the optimal organizational setup for conducting strategy formulation, budget planning, and budget execution? What would be the relationship between recurrent and capital expenditures? What would be the relationship with sector ministries and other stakeholders?

After the ouster of President Suharto, Indonesians started a national debate on the type of planning system that would be a consistent move toward decentralization and more inclusive economic and political systems. New laws were passed to restructure the roles and functions of the Indonesian ministries of planning, national development planning, and finance. Similarly, Prime Minister Modi of India on

January 1, 2015, scrapped the powerful planning commission of India and replaced it with a policy think tank, NITI Aayog, which involves states in economic policymaking. The moves in Indonesia and India to reduce the role of central planning agencies reflect a trend toward greater decentralization, as well as the bigger role of the private sector in the economy. Decentralization is not advanced in the Arab world, and there are few structured public-private dialogues. Therefore, it may make sense to first concentrate on making the central economic agencies function more effectively and efficiently while becoming more open and inclusive.

Effective implementation needs accountability. Naturally, each executing agency in charge of a particular sector or policy issue should be held accountable for implementation. But there also needs to be a supervisory mechanism that secures the accountability of the institutions and ensures that things happen. The Iraq case study has shown that peer pressure can be a powerful tool for encouraging responsible agencies, policymakers, and leaders to accelerate implementation. Reviewing implementation progress with peers provides an incentive for institutions to improve performance to avoid public embarrassment.

In addition to pressure from their peers, institutions could respond to pressure from the top (president or prime minister) and from the bottom (citizens). In Morocco, the execution of sector strategies (for tourism, industry, agriculture, and so on) has been boosted by the direct involvement of the king in the supervision of the implementation process. Beneficiaries of government programs could also exert pressure to ensure implementation, but they need to be organized so that their voices are heard. In Brazil, nongovernmental organizations were encouraged to help organize the various stakeholders and citizen groups who benefited from the Zero Hunger Program.

The insufficiency of resources is often blamed for inadequate implementation. Effective use of financial and human resources is essential for effective and efficient implementation. The case study of urban transport in Egypt suggests ways of dealing with financial resource constraints through better prioritization, improved cost recovery, and private sector participation. Constraint on financial resources tends to be highlighted as a major implementation gap in developing countries, but as this discussion indicates, there are ways of dealing with this problem.

The Iraq case study highlights capacity and knowledge constraints. The solution to Iraqi officials' lack of experience in implementing donor-supported programs was to intensify contacts between donor and recipient to facilitate knowledge transfer and to share experiences. Moreover, international agencies (the UNDP, in the case of Iraq) can be helpful in building capacity and providing technical support.

Effective monitoring and evaluation systems are needed to increase the impact and quality of public investment and to promote better service delivery to the public. Such systems help improve institutional capacity and accountability. Some countries (for example, the Philippines, Indonesia, and Malaysia) have been trying to strengthen monitoring and evaluation through the introduction of results-based management and budgeting as well as through the adoption of key performance indicators for the public sector.

Both the Philippines and Indonesia made significant progress in establishing results-based public sector management and performance-based budgeting, where linkage between planning and budgeting was strengthened. Both installed a medium-term expenditure framework and set performance indicators to be monitored during implementation. In the case of Indonesia, the president established a unit to monitor the progress of achieved results, and incentives and sanctions were set to enhance performance. As noted earlier, in Malaysia a whole machinery for monitoring and evaluating the implementation of five-year plans has been set up and is managed by the Implementation Coordination Unit, a special unit that reports directly to the prime minister.

Successful political and economic transitions require renewed institutions that are responsive to citizens' demand and are able to efficiently implement plans and projects. The Arab countries in transition need to pay particular attention to the development of effective economic institutions that are responsible for project and program implementation and public service delivery. Experiences from East Asia and Latin America indicate that successful implementation of economic development programs almost always requires institutional strengthening and renewal.

5

Entrepreneurship for Inclusion

While strengthening public institutions responsible for implementing economic policies and important projects that provide physical and social infrastructure is necessary, it is always important to remember that it is the private sector that creates jobs and income-generating opportunities for youth. Economic growth in the Arab countries in transition has not been inclusive, as it left millions of people stuck in the lower middle class consuming $2 to $6 a day and provided few opportunities for youth who felt economically and socially excluded. Therefore, encouraging youth entrepreneurship and the development of small businesses has to be central to any new growth strategy.

Arab economies are dominated by large firms and by micro enterprises that mostly operate in the informal sector. Those micro enterprises use low technology and therefore provide low wages and are predominantly family affairs. They provide livelihoods for large numbers of Arabs, but they do not offer decent jobs. While poor and uneducated youth have no option but to work in the informal sector, educated youth prefer to wait for a formal job. This could explain why youth unemployment rates in ACTs increase with the level of education. Moreover, the informal sector is considered unsafe for women, because of the high incidence of sexual harassment. Unable to find formal jobs and denied entry into the informal sector, many women are discouraged and remain at home. Inclusive growth can be achieved by shifting away from a system that favors large and established enterprises to one that focuses on developing small businesses and on creating more opportunities for young men and women.

Micro, Small, and Medium-Size Enterprises in the Arab Countries in Transition

A focus on expanding small businesses and the small and medium-size enterprise (SME) sector would appear to be an appropriate response to the need to grow the middle class and provide greater opportunities for young men and women as business people as well as employees. The development of small and medium-size enterprises is closely linked to economic growth. In developed countries, 50 percent of GDP, on average, is produced by SMEs. Among the member nations of the Organization for Economic Cooperation and Development, SMEs (those with fewer than 250 employees) are responsible for two-thirds of total employment and 60 percent of industrial employment. Small and medium-size enterprises are often on the cutting edge of innovation, as their small size allows them to be more flexible and attentive to their client needs than larger businesses.[1]

Figure 5-1 shows employment shares by size of enterprise.[2] It seems clear from the graph that Arab SMEs do not play the same role in employment creation as their Western counterparts. Their share in total employment rarely exceeds 20–30 percent. Most employment is created in micro enterprises, with large enterprises also making significant contributions of about 30 percent of total employment in countries like Jordan and Tunisia. That is why some analysts often talk about the missing middle in the world of Arab enterprises. Micro enterprises (those with fewer than ten employees) appear to be the most important employers in the region, responsible for nearly 60 percent of total employment in Egypt and West Bank–Gaza and about 40 percent in Tunisia and Jordan.

What are these micro enterprises that employ so many young Arabs? Ghanem (2013) uses a simple enterprise classification system, widely accepted in Egypt, which is based on number of employees. According to this classification, micro enterprises are defined as those that employ

1. See Ardic, Mylenko, and Saltane (2011).
2. The graph shows the share of employment by firm size according to the following classification: micro firms have less than 5 employees, small firms have between 5 and 9 employees, medium firms have between 10 and 99 employees, and large firms have 100 employees or more.

FIGURE 5-1. SMEs and Job Creation in the Arab World

Percent

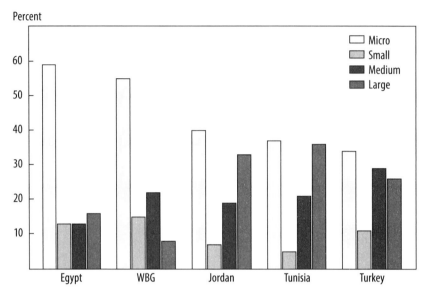

Source: World Bank (2015). Periods covered, by country: Turkey, 2006; Tunisia, 1996–2010; Jordan, 2006; Egypt, 2006; Palestine, 2004, 2007, 2012.

fewer than 10 workers, small enterprises employ 10–49 workers, medium-size enterprises employ 50–99 workers, and large enterprises employ 100 workers and more. Egyptian micro enterprises are mostly family businesses that provide simple services to the household sector, using traditional technologies, with low capital-to-labor ratios and low productivity (and hence wages). More than 60 percent of employees are related to the owner-manager. Slightly fewer than two-thirds of micro enterprises work in trade. These are small retailers and wholesalers who sell food products, clothes, furniture, plastics, and building materials. About 30 percent operate in the services sector, including transportation and distribution, laundry, cafes, restaurants, and hotels. Fewer than 10 percent of micro enterprises are in manufacturing, including food processing, wood and furniture, ceramics, building materials, and some electrical and engineering workshops.

Looking at Tunisia, Boughzala (2013) argues that the informal sector, consisting mainly of micro enterprises, is the largest and the fastest growing of private enterprises. The number of informal micro enterprises is growing annually at 5.1 percent compared with 2.1 percent for the larger enterprises. According to Boughzala, Tunisian micro enterprises are the least structured, are the most volatile and uncertain, and generate mostly low-quality, informal jobs. Micro enterprises cover a large spectrum of activities but are concentrated in food, retail commerce, construction, transportation, and automobile repair. Tunisian micro firms have limited access to formal financing, which covers less than 10 percent of their investment, and depend mainly on self-financing. Like their Egyptian counterparts, Tunisian micro enterprises have limited access to new technology: more than 90 percent of these businesses lack access to the Internet and consequently have low productivity and offer low wages.

The situation seems to be the same in Algeria, where a 2011 census of 200,000 SMEs showed that 95 percent of them are informal micro enterprises providing low-quality services to households. It therefore seems that the Arab micro enterprise sector mostly plays a social role as a coping and livelihood mechanism for the large proportion of the population that is unable to find opportunities in the formal public or private sectors. These businesses are unlikely to be the basis for a new and dynamic SME sector that can innovate and compete on the world markets.

Nevertheless, there are a few success stories in the Arab world. Stone and Badawy (2011) present cases of Arab SMEs whose sales or employment increased by at least 20 percent between 2003 and 2007. They find that those enterprises are more innovative, hire more-qualified personnel, invest more in staff training, and use the Internet more intensively. Many of those enterprises operate under licensing agreements with foreign companies, have access to foreign technology, and obtain international quality certification. This implies that the success of Arab SMEs requires investment in human resources, in information and communications technology, and in quality assurance mechanisms.

Surveys and interviews with entrepreneurs in Algeria, Egypt, and Tunisia indicate that the Arab SME sector faces six important challenges: access to markets, access to technologies, access to financing, access to land and infrastructure, a constraining legal and regulatory framework, and weak governance and lack of accountability.[3] These constraints prevent the Arab SMEs from growing into a vibrant private sector that provides much needed employment to youth and women.

3. For Algeria, see Berrah and Boukriff (2013) and Gharbi (2011). For Egypt, see Ghanem (2013), and for Tunisia, see Boughzala (2013).

Access to markets for sufficient quantities at a remunerative price is essential for the success of any business. Most of the Arab SMEs surveyed operate mainly in local markets with no links to national or international markets. They are unaware of consumer tastes in those larger markets and do not know how to access them.

Enterprises also need appropriate up-to-date technologies to produce the needed goods and deliver them to the market. Typically this would require importing the technology in the form of machinery and equipment, licensing agreements, and so on. In some countries this is a problem, because it involves dealing with customs rules and regulations. In Algeria, some businessmen also stated that controls made it difficult to obtain foreign exchange to pay for the imported equipment and licenses. After purchasing the technology, firms need to develop training programs for their staff, as most SMEs in the Arab world have little experience with modern technologies.

Most SMEs around the world complain that access to financing is a major constraint, and Arab SMEs are no exception. Algerian businessmen complain that the banks refuse to lend to SMEs that they consider too risky, and at the same time microfinance institutions are ill adapted to the needs of medium-size enterprises. Surveys in Egypt indicate that only 2.3 percent of entrepreneurs were able to get a formal loan in order to start their business, and 2.9 percent obtained an informal loan.[4]

Small businesses also complain about access to land and to infrastructure. In Algeria, 35 percent of investor requests from government concern access to industrial land. Algerian SMEs complain about the lack of information concerning the availability of land for industrial development, a rigid application of real estate rules, and failure to regularize land titles. In Egypt, lack of access to infrastructure and public services affects the performance of all enterprises but particularly small ones that do not have the resources to invest in alternatives to publicly provided infrastructure.

Arab legal and regulatory frameworks discourage SME development. As a result, the rate of creation of new formal enterprises in the Arab world (excluding Gulf Cooperation Council members) is the lowest in the world. In Algeria, Egypt, Iraq, and Syria, the rate of creation of new limited liability companies is less than 0.5 for each 1,000 inhabitants

---

4. MSE survey carried out by the Economic Research Forum in 2003.

of economically active age. For comparison purposes, the average for developing countries is 1.7 and the average for the whole world is 2.6. Surveys in Egypt show that about two-thirds of entrepreneurs consider the tax system (rates and administration) to be a major impediment to their work, and a somewhat lower proportion (60 percent) say the same about licensing and registration requirements.

The Micro and Small Enterprise Sector in Egypt

Only 28 percent of Egyptian youth find formal sector jobs—18 percent in the public sector and 10 percent in the formal private sector. The vast majority, 72 percent, end up working in the informal micro and small enterprise (MSE) sector, often as unpaid family workers. For those who are paid, many have no labor contract, no job security, and no social benefits.

According to a 2006 Establishment Census conducted by the Central Agency for Public Mobilization and Statistics, the Egyptian labor force is estimated at about 20.1 million workers, with about 7 million working for the public sector and the remainder divided nearly evenly between agriculture and the nonagriculture private sector.[5] There are 2.5 million nonagricultural private enterprises in Egypt employing 7.3 million workers. Micro and small enterprises (with fewer than fifty workers each) represent nearly 99 percent of total private enterprises and about 80 percent of total employment (5.8 million workers). Furthermore, of those 5.8 million workers, 88 percent are employed by micro enterprises, with 72 percent employed in enterprises with one to four workers and 16 percent in enterprises with five to nine workers. The remaining 18 percent are employed by small enterprises that employ ten to forty-nine workers. This relative importance of small and micro enterprises for employment generation is not unique to Egypt. For example, Ozar, Ozartan, and Irfanoglu (2008) and Samitowska (2011) show similar results for Turkey and Poland, respectively.[6]

5. Quoted in el-Mahdi (2012).

6. Data for this section on Egypt are taken from two sources: an MSE survey carried out by the Economic Research Forum in 2003 that covered 4,957 enterprises and a survey of 3,000 enterprises carried out in 2010 and 2011 and reviewed by el-Mahdi (2012) in a background paper for the Brookings project on Arab economies. Whenever possible, I base my results on the more recent survey. However, the 2003 survey is larger and covers more questions.

TABLE 5-1. Overview of MSE Sector, Egypt, 2003

Category	Average assets[a]	Average employment[b]	Education of entrepreneur[c]
Total	30,147	2.2	8.4
Youth (15 to 24 years of age) entrepreneur	16,809	2.3	10.3
Youth and female entrepreneur	18,368	2.4	11.2

Source: Author's calculations from ERF 2003 survey.
a. In Egyptian pounds (LE).
b. Number of workers.
c. Years of formal schooling.

The vast majority of MSEs in Egypt are very small, with average assets valued at 30,000 Egyptian pounds (LE) (some US$5,000) and average employment of 2.2 workers (see table 5-1). The average age of the owner-manager of an enterprise is 40.3 years, with an average education level of 8.4 years of formal schooling. Women entrepreneurs head about 10.5 percent of enterprises. About 12 percent of entrepreneurs are young, between the ages of fifteen and twenty-four. Enterprises headed by youth tend to have fewer assets (nearly half as much) than the average. Another important feature of young entrepreneurs is that they tend to be better educated than older colleagues, with an average education of 10.3 years. In fact, the simple correlation coefficient between age and years of education for the whole sample is −0.33. Some 15.4 percent of young entrepreneurs are women. They tend to be better educated than their male counterparts, and their enterprises tend to be slightly bigger. Table 5-2 shows the age structure of entrepreneurs from the 2011 survey. Youth, defined as younger than twenty-five years of age, represent only 10 percent of the sample. However, as table 5-2 also shows, if the definition of youth is extended to include all of those younger than thirty, then young entrepreneurs would represent about 23 percent of total entrepreneurs.

Young people's share of employment in MSEs is much higher than their share in ownership. Using data from the 2003 Economic Research Forum survey, I estimate that those in the fifteen to twenty-four age group represent 37 percent of total MSE employment. If we define youth as being younger than thirty, then this share rises to more than 50 percent. Women's employment in MSEs remains low, at only 11.4 percent, as those enterprises are not considered safe for female workers. Half of

TABLE 5-2. Enterprises, by Sex and Age of Entrepreneur, Egypt, 2011

Percent

Age	Male	Female	Total
Less than 18 years	0.2	0.8	0.2
18 to less than 21 years	2.0	4.1	2.2
21 to less than 25 years	7.4	9.6	7.6
25 to less than 30 years	12.9	13.0	12.9
30 to less than 40 years	27.2	21.2	26.6
40 years or more	50.4	51.3	50.5

Source: El-Mahdi (2012).

the women working in MSEs (50.1 percent in the Economic Research Forum 2003 sample) are younger than twenty-five. Wages are low, the average wage for male workers in the 2011 survey being $3.70 a day and that for female workers $2.60 a day. Slightly more than half (50.5 percent in the 2003 survey) of employees have a work contract, which shows the precarious nature of employment in this sector.

Egyptian MSEs mostly provide services to the household sector. In response to a question about their main clients, 90 percent of enterprises service households, 8 percent sell to other firms or home-based workers, and 2 percent sell to government or public enterprises. Thus it is evident that little subcontracting is taking place. More than 99 percent of MSEs sell mainly to local markets, with few selling in the national market (within Egypt). Only 0.3 percent of enterprises sell to the export market.

Peattie (1987, p. 851) states that the concept of an informal sector is "utterly fuzzy," and this seems to be the case in Egypt, where most MSEs operate in a gray zone between formality and informality. To be considered formal an Egyptian enterprise needs to have a business license, be registered as a commercial or industrial establishment, obtain a tax card, and keep regular accounts. Noncompliance with one or more of those four official procedures would make the enterprise count as informal. Table 5-3 shows the status of compliance in the 2011 sample. Only 21.6 percent of enterprises comply with all four procedures and are therefore considered formal. On the other extreme, 18.4 percent do not comply with any procedure and therefore operate completely informally. The remaining 60 percent of enterprises comply

TABLE 5-3. MSE Compliance with Official Procedures, Egypt, 2011
Percent

Procedure	MSEs complying
Business license	66.4
Commercial or industrial registration	70.1
Tax card	73.1
Keeping regular accounts	28.4

Source: El-Mahdi (2012).

with one or more (45 percent of the total comply with three of the four) of the procedures and are officially considered informal, but in fact seem to be at least partially formal. The procedure that is least complied with is (unsurprisingly) maintaining regular accounts and presenting them to the tax department (see table 5-3). The degree of formality is positively correlated with the size of the enterprise and the education level of its owner, and urban-based enterprises tend to be more formal than rural-based ones. Similar results on the relationship between characteristics of the entrepreneur and formality and firm size were found by Jackle and Li (2006) for Peru.

Micro and small enterprises have very low capital-labor ratios and tend to use simple traditional technologies. The average capital-labor ratio calculated from the 2003 survey is around LE 10,000 (about US$1,600) and LE 14,000 (about US$2,300) from the 2011 survey. The surveys asked entrepreneurs about the type of technology they use, including the choice between traditional, modern, and up to date. Among the manufacturing enterprises, 68 percent stated that they use traditional technology, while 30 percent use modern technology and only 2 percent use up-to-date technology. In services the shares were 71 percent traditional, 27 percent modern, and 2 percent up to date; while the shares in the trade sector were 80 percent, 19 percent, and 1 percent respectively. Thirty percent of entrepreneurs stated that they introduced innovations to their services and products to meet changing market needs. A 2008 survey on innovation covered 3,000 manufacturing and services enterprises.[7] It found that 19 percent of enterprises had technological innovation activities, with manufacturing firms

7. Egyptian National Innovation Survey, 2008.

TABLE 5-4. Source of Initial Funding, Egypt, 2003

Percent

	All entrepreneurs	Youth entrepreneurs
Formal loan	2.3	1.4
Informal loan	2.9	2.2
Individual savings	68.6	73.7
Inheritance	20.2	18.7
Others	6.0	4.0

Source: Author's calculations from 2003 ERF survey.

and larger firms being more likely to innovate. About 90 percent of innovations were produced within the firm, and only 10 percent were produced in collaboration with domestic or foreign partners.

When asked why they did not use modern technology, more than half of the entrepreneurs stated that they could not afford the expense. Table 5-4 shows sources of funding for MSE start-ups. It indicates that only 1.4 percent of youth entrepreneurs were able to get a formal loan to start their business, and 2.2 percent obtained informal loans. Most entrepreneurs (68.6 percent of total and 73.7 percent of youth) relied on their own savings to start their business. Inheritance is also an important source of financing, with 20.2 percent of entrepreneurs (18.7 percent of youth) stating that they used money that they inherited to start their business.

Access to infrastructure and public services is an important factor affecting the performance of MSEs. Table 5-5 presents the proportion of entrepreneurs who answered no in response to questions about access to different types of infrastructure. A surprising finding here is the high proportion that does not have access to landline telephones (71.9 percent of the total and 73 percent of youth). However, it is not clear how serious this is at a time of increasing access to mobile phones. Public transport for people and goods appears as a major problem for MSEs, with some 95 percent of them stating that they do not have access to those services. The same is true for water and sewage, as 59.4 percent of respondents stated that they had no access to water and 68.1 percent have no access to sewage. There does not appear to be a significant difference between young entrepreneurs and the rest of the sample in terms of access to infrastructure and public services.

TABLE 5-5. Access to Infrastructure, Egypt, 2003[a]

Category	All entrepreneurs	Young entrepreneurs
Water	59.4	57.2
Electricity	6.7	5.7
Telephone	71.9	73.0
Sewage	68.1	67.2
Roads	10.8	9.9
Transport of workers	96.6	97.1
Transport of goods	94.8	95.4

Source: Author's calculations from 2003 ERF survey.
a. Table presents share of surveyed entrepreneurs reporting that they have no access to item.

Two-thirds of small-firm entrepreneurs identified taxation (tax rates as well as tax administration) as a key constraint facing their business development (table 5-6). This is consistent with the earlier finding that the vast majority of small firms did not comply with the requirement to file their accounts with the tax department. It is commonplace for businessmen all over the world to complain about taxes. Nevertheless, the loud complaints (based on 2003 data) and massive noncompliance (based on 2011 data) may be an indication that a review of tax policies affecting small businesses is warranted. About 61 percent of all entrepreneurs (64 percent of young entrepreneurs) mentioned licensing and registration as key constraints. This is surprising since in the 2003 survey about 70 percent of respondents report having complied with those requirements. During 2004–10 the government, as part of its economic reform program, embarked on a massive deregulation and simplification effort. Hence this conclusion could be based on data from an earlier period. However, el-Mahdi (2012) states that the deregulation and simplification effort does not seem to have affected the MSE sector, based on a 2011 survey. Hence there may be two explanations for this result: the entrepreneurs may be ill informed and unaware of the changes or application of the deregulation and simplification measures is being ignored by a bureaucracy that is keen to protect possible sources of rents.

Table 5-6 also indicates that financing is seen as a major constraint by nearly 65 percent of entrepreneurs (61 percent of youth). More-detailed data on access to credit are presented in table 5-7, which shows

TABLE 5-6. Constraints on Small Business, Egypt, 2003[a]

Constraint	All entrepreneurs	Young entrepreneurs
Securing capital	64.6	62.1
Licensing and registration	61.3	64.0
Labor law	32.3	35.7
Labor inspection	44.9	49.2
Tax rates	68.6	66.7
Customs duties	5.8	5.8
Tax administration	65.0	63.0

Source: Author's calculations from ERF 2003 survey.
a. Table presents share of surveyed entrepreneurs reporting the item is a major constraint.

TABLE 5-7. Credit to Small Businesses, 2003
Percent

Category	All entrepreneurs	Young entrepreneurs
Access to credit	5.3	4.8
Source of credit		
Friends and family, business associates	47.9	57.1
Bank	35.6	28.6
Social Development Fund	9.2	3.6
Nongovernmental organization	7.3	10.7

Source: Author's calculations from 2003 ERF survey.

that only 5.3 percent of entrepreneurs said they have had any access to credit, and of those, 47.9 percent (57.1 percent of youth) received that credit from family, friends, or business associates. Banks provided 35.6 percent of credit to MSEs, while the Social Fund for Development and nongovernmental organizations provided 9.2 and 7.3 percent, respectively. The table also shows that young entrepreneurs have much less access to credit from banks and the Social Fund for Development than older ones.

The surveys indicate a significant level of dissatisfaction with government policies affecting small businesses. Entrepreneurs claim that the regulatory framework (licensing, registration, and so on) is a hindrance, that it costs significant time and money, that taxation is high and cumbersome, and that they have little access to basic infrastructure or to credit. Very few seem to have benefited from targeted interventions such as credit from the Social Development Fund or special training programs. Hence there seems to be a good case for a review of policies and programs that affect small enterprises in Egypt.

Tunisian Private Sector

Most observers rank Tunisia better than Egypt in terms of the business environment, and the country implemented many reforms over the two decades preceding the Arab Spring.[8] Nevertheless, private sector investment remained low at about 15 percent of GDP. Moreover, growth was not sufficient and did not create enough jobs for the young Tunisians entering the labor market, especially those with higher education. Table 5-8 shows that the unemployment rate increased with education, and Tunisians with higher education had an unemployment rate of about 29 percent by May 2011.

As in the case of Egypt, there appears to have been a significant gap between official rules and regulations and actual implementation. The business environment has been plagued with cronyism and corruption, and was not conducive to substantial investment and enterprise creation, especially small and medium enterprises (SMEs). Private investments remained at the bottom of the technological scale. Most Tunisian firms failed to move up the value chain or to improve their productivity. They were unable to switch from labor-intensive, low-wage activities to more capital- and skill-intensive ones, which could explain the low demand for educated labor.

Also as in Egypt, the informal sector, which mainly consists of micro enterprises, is important for providing livelihood to a large portion of the population. Surveys indicate that 98 percent of micro enterprises employ no more than two persons and of these 87 percent employ only one individual (the owner). Total employment of the informal micro enterprise sector is slightly more than 500,000 people, 80 percent of whom are men. This is about 16 percent of the country's total workforce and only about 5 percent of wage-earning employees, making a little less than the minimum legal wage (less than TND 250 per month

8. For example, see any edition of the World Bank's Doing Business Report. Tunisia is always ranked better than Egypt.

TABLE 5-8. Unemployment Rate, by Education Level, Tunisia, Various Years

Education	2005	2007	2009	May 2011
None	6.3	4.4	6.1	8.0
Primary	14.3	11.5	10.4	12.4
Secondary	13.3	13.5	14.0	20.6
Higher	14.0	18.2	21.9	29.2

Source: Boughzala (2013).

in 2007) and often without any social security. Female employees earn 30 percent less than male employees, and wage is positively correlated with the size of the enterprise.[9]

The nature of the Tunisian micro enterprise sector could explain why unemployment increases with the level of education. This is the most dynamic and fastest growing sector, but it only provides low-productivity, low-paying jobs. Educated youth are not attracted to those informal micro enterprises. They prefer to wait for a formal sector job, and most of them have families that can support them while waiting. Hence they remain unemployed for long periods of time. Youth with less education, who typically are from poorer families, cannot afford this luxury. Informal jobs in micro enterprises are the only available source of livelihood. Hence their unemployment rate is low, but so is the quality of their jobs. In general, poorer youth are forced to join the informal sector, even if they are educated. Mohamed Bouazizi, the vegetable salesman who burnt himself in despair and sparked the Arab Spring, is an example of this group of young people.

The Tunisian case also highlights the plight of young Arab women. Tunisian women have as much access to education as men. In fact, more young women graduate from universities than young men. But most of those young women either drop out of the labor force or remain unemployed. Women avoid the informal sector because it is considered inhospitable to women. Survey data indicate that young women prefer to respect themselves and stay at home rather than seek informal employment. The public sector used to offer good jobs to women, but its hiring has declined due to budget constraints and the necessity to provide space for private sector development. The formal private sector

9. Data in this section are from Boughzala (2013).

is not growing fast enough to provide enough jobs for all young people, and when offered a choice between hiring a young man or a young woman most prefer hiring the man. Data from the World Values Survey indicate that across the Arab world a majority of people feel that it is more important for men to have jobs than women, because men must provide for their families.

In Tunisia, SMEs are 2.5 percent of the total number of firms, but they generate about one-third of total employment and have 43 percent of salaried employees. Small enterprises (between 10 and 50 employees), which are by far the majority among SMEs, maintain many informal features, in particular in their human resources management, while larger enterprises behave more like modern and formal enterprises. The larger the size the closer they are to formality. Since half of the Tunisian SMEs are small and employ fewer than 20 persons and 25 percent employ between 20 and 50 persons, informality is widespread among SMEs. In 2010 only 2,613 enterprises out of 11,242 SMEs employed between 50 and 200 persons each and qualified as medium enterprises.

However, SMEs have not been growing fast enough. According to the World Bank (2015), this could be explained in part by a distorted policy environment that aimed at protecting a few large firms that had political connections to the Ben Ali regime. The system generated privileges for the lucky few and did not create a level playing field. According to the World Bank, policy and regulatory framework insulated politically connected firms from domestic as well as international competition. Small and medium-size firms were not allowed to enter sectors where politically connected firms operated, and when they did enter those sectors they were always at a competitive disadvantage that ensured that they remained small and could not grow.

The Way Forward

Achieving inclusive growth requires a fundamental change in Arab economic policies affecting the private sector. Past policies that prioritized large projects at the expense of small and medium projects may have succeeded in achieving high growth rates. However, they led to widespread dissatisfaction, and eventually revolution, because large segments of the population did not benefit from that growth. One could argue that given enough time the benefits from growth would have "trickled down" to the middle and poorer classes. But such a process would take decades to take its course, if it actually works at all. Hence it is not a politically feasible option. Developing small and medium-size businesses should be a priority.

The aim of policy should not be simply to support the growth of the existing SME sector, which consists mostly of micro enterprises. It should aim to transform it by raising its productivity and its linkages to domestic and international markets. The objective should be to support the modernization of the sector so that it can become more dynamic, provide better living standards for young entrepreneurs and decent jobs for new entrants to the labor market. A possible vision would be to become similar to the sectors in Europe or Japan where SMEs lead in innovation, often operate in clusters, and have strong links to larger firms as well as to national and international markets.

Governments cannot provide all of the solutions on their own. nongovernmental organizations around the world usually play a significant role in supporting SMEs. They help mobilize resources and provide credit to the sector, from their own resources as well as working as delivery agents for public agencies. They are also in a good position to provide technical and marketing support, and to help organize broad consultations with relevant stakeholders. Governments can help develop NGOs by putting in place appropriate legal and regulatory frameworks.[10]

The World Bank (2015) argues that the main problem holding back the development of the Arab formal private sector, including SMEs, is a policy environment that favors a few large firms that are well-connected to political elites and insulates them from competition. The development of a modern and competitive SME sector will require the creation of a level playing field so that newcomers can compete with the older and well-established market players. That is, the close and nontransparent ties between political and business elites need to be severed. Political changes after the Arab Spring revolutions, and the departure of long-serving autocrats like presidents Ben Ali and Mubarak and the political and business elites surrounding them, are a step toward weakening those ties. However, unless institutional and regulatory changes are adopted, there is always a risk that new alliances between

10. See Kharas and Abdou (2012) for a study of NGO development in Egypt.

politicians and large business interests will emerge to the detriment of small and medium activities.

Arab SMEs complain about high tax rates and cumbersome tax administration. High and complicated tax systems could also be a way of discriminating against small businesses. Large and well-connected firms are better able to deal with the tax department and are therefore at an advantage compared to SMEs. This advantage is positively correlated with the level of taxation and the degree of complication. Hence an important way of supporting SME development is to lower taxes and simplify the tax system. International experience indicates that this is an important area for reform. According to the World Bank (2015), many countries (for example, Gabon, Jamaica, and Sweden) have reduced profit taxes for SMEs by 2 percentage points or more, while others (for example, Guatemala, Croatia, Philippines) have simplified tax compliance by introducing systems of electronic filing and payment.

Most new jobs are created by start-ups rather than by the expansion of existing SMEs. This is true around the world, and the Arab countries are no exception.[11] That is why it is important that entrepreneurs not be discouraged from opening new businesses by excessive bureaucracy. Moreover, survey data indicate that the difficulty in obtaining official permits and licenses is one of the reasons why some SMEs prefer to remain informal.[12] Some countries (for example, Algeria and Egypt) are trying to facilitate the process for entrepreneurs by putting in place one-stop shops that handle all procedures and obtain all permits on behalf of the entrepreneurs. But so far experience with one-stop shops has been mixed, and many small businesspeople face long delays at the start-up phase, which obviously puts them at a disadvantage versus the large well-connected businesses who are able to maneuver the bureaucracy and obtain all of the required permits in a timely fashion.

Restrictions on international trade are important impediments to the development of SMEs in the Arab world. SMEs need to be able to import equipment and intermediate inputs as well as technology and know-how in order to be internationally competitive. Moreover, many successful SMEs enter the export market. High import tariffs as well as

---

11. World Bank (2015, p. 72).

12. See Ghanem (2013) for the example of Egypt and Boughzala (2013) for the example of Tunisia.

complicated customs procedures are an important constraint on SMEs in some Arab countries, for example, Algeria. In other countries (for example, Egypt) access to foreign exchange in order to pay for imported goods and services is the key constraint. Cognizant of the importance of international trade for SME development, many countries (for example, Argentina and Mexico) have simplified their import procedures and strengthened capacity of their customs and ports authorities.[13]

Good tax laws and simple regulations will only be effective if their implementation is not marred by abuse and corruption. Hence efforts to fight corruption and to professionalize the civil service could have a positive impact on SME development. Government needs to partner with civil society, the press, and business owners to bring about greater transparency and hold civil servants accountable. During its transition, Indonesia created the Partnership for Governance Reform between government and civil society to lead the fight against corruption.

Direct interventions by governments to support SMEs should go beyond credit programs to include support to some pilot SME clusters and programs for entrepreneurship development. Cluster development could be a very useful activity, provided that it is based on an existing local competence. Initially, interventions could focus on supporting local SMEs to better connect with each other, modernize, and link to national and international markets. For such an endeavor to succeed, it would be important to partner with a private enterprise that can provide the technical support and market access. Bringing in a foreign partner would be particularly useful for export-oriented activities.

Governments should also consider policies to encourage foreign investors to partner with domestic SMEs to help them obtain technical design and marketing expertise. In the case of the garment industry in Bali, the Indonesian government reduced the minimum level of foreign investment from $1 million to $250,000 in order to encourage small foreign investors to partner with local SMEs, bringing in their technical know-how and market access.

A key challenge to the implementation of the vision presented here is that young Arabs are not prepared for a life of entrepreneurship and risk taking. Education systems in the Arab world have been geared to produce civil servants and do not provide graduates with the skills

13. World Bank (2014b, p. 107).

needed to survive in a twenty-first-century marketplace. Educated Arab youth do not have the skills or the inclination to start their own business. They prefer the security of a public sector job even if it implies a long period of unemployment as they wait for a job opening. There is clearly a need to modernize Arab education. At the same time governments can partner with the private sector to develop entrepreneurship programs to provide skills to youth and help them start their own business.

6

Targeting Excluded Groups:
Youth, Smallholder Farmers, and Women

Economic exclusion was an important driver for the Arab Spring revolts. Although the Arab economies grew at decent rates in the decade preceding the revolution, large groups of people were not part of this growth and did not benefit from it. The three biggest excluded groups were youth, family farmers, and women. Redressing grievances of these groups and including them in future economic plans is essential for long-term sustainability of Arab economies.

Youth is a large excluded group. The old social contract whereby government provided free education, guaranteed public sector jobs, and subsidized housing and consumer goods has imploded. Governments are no longer able to provide jobs to all graduates or to subsidize housing and consumer goods. To benefit from economic growth, get married, and raise a family, youth need to find decent jobs in the private sector that allow them to pay full prices for housing and consumer goods, or they need to start their own small business. However, the education system was designed to produce civil servants, not private sector workers or entrepreneurs. That is why it needs to be overhauled. Unless curricula and pedagogical methods are modernized youth will remain excluded from economic gains.

Smallholder farmers are another excluded group. Whole regions in the Arab world are excluded from the benefits of growth, and those regions are nearly all rural and highly dependent on agriculture. Moreover, most agricultural plots are small in size and are managed by smallholder family farmers. Hence policies aimed at achieving inclusive growth need to include special programs and measures to support smallholders.

Arab women (including young women and women farmers) suffer more than men from exclusion. They have lower labor force participation rates, higher unemployment rates, and limited access to credit, land, and other productive assets. That is why programs that target women are also critical for achieving inclusive growth.

Education as Key to Ending Youth Exclusion

Policies to deal with the problem of youth exclusion have usually focused on raising the demand for labor by encouraging more private sector activities, especially start-ups and SMEs, or by expanding the public sector. Demand-side policies are important, but they may not be sufficient to expand youth opportunities and ensure that youth are not excluded from the benefits of economic growth. The skills that Arab youth acquire at schools and universities do not seem to match those required by employers. And the education systems in the Arab world do not prepare students for a life of entrepreneurship and risk taking.

Arab countries have made huge strides in expanding access to education, and more young Arabs than ever before are attending schools and universities. Arab governments spend more than 5 percent of GDP on education, which is a higher share than other middle-income regions spend. They have demonstrated a commitment to education and have succeeded in increasing the quantity of education delivered by schools and universities.

Quality of education should be the focus now. There is a need to improve the teaching of basic literacy and numeracy skills and to adjust curricula and teaching methods to reflect the skills and competencies demanded by today's globalized labor market. There is also a need for institutional reforms that hold schools and teachers accountable for student learning.

Arab countries have done particularly well in improving primary school enrollment. Morocco, Oman, Djibouti, Mauritania, and Yemen made the largest improvements over the first decade of this century. As these same countries had the lowest rates of primary enrollment in the region in 2002, this indicates a strong narrowing of disparities in access across the region. Despite impressive gains, three of these countries—Djibouti, Mauritania, and Yemen—continue to have the lowest enrollment rates in the region. For instance, while primary enrollment in Djibouti

FIGURE 6-1. Primary Net Enrollment Rate, Selected Arab Countries, 2002–11

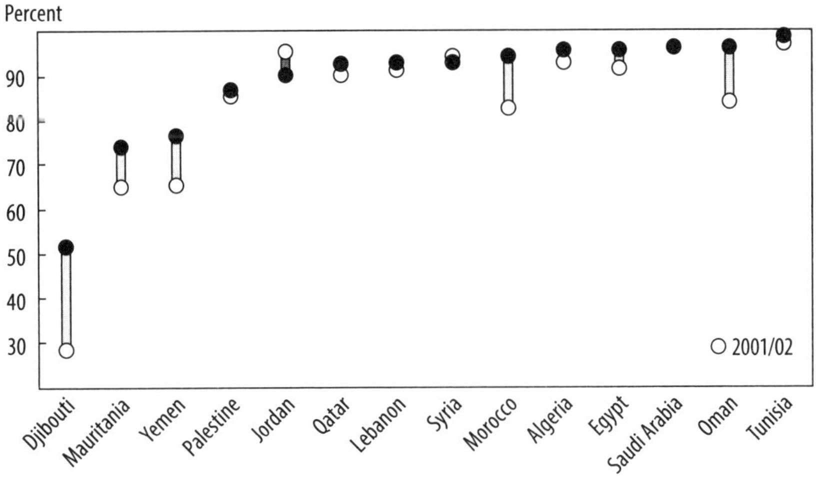

Source: UNESCO Institute for Statistics database.

has jumped nearly 30 percentage points since 2002, as of 2010–11 it rests at just 52 percent—by far lowest in the region (figure 6-1).

Secondary enrollment has also improved significantly, though these data are much more limited. In the five countries for which ten-year trends can be calculated, all have recorded positive gains at the secondary level. In particular, Syria, Oman, and Qatar have made impressive progress, with enrollment gains of 26, 24, and 12 percentage points, respectively, although Syria has most likely lost much of this progress over the past three years of civil conflict (figure 6-2).[1]

Increasing school attendance is an important achievement, but it does not necessarily mean that students are prepared to be competitive in a globalized twenty-first-century marketplace. Nor does it necessarily mean that they are acquiring the skills that prospective employers are looking for. In fact, an important critique of Arab education systems is that they were designed to produce public sector workers and do not reflect today's realities, where the public sector is stagnating or declining and most new jobs are in the private sector.

A fairly obvious weakness of Arab education systems is that they tend to overproduce people with higher education in arts and humanities,

1. For more detail see Steer, Ghanem, and Jalbout (2014).

FIGURE 6-2. Secondary Net Enrollment Rate, Selected Arab Countries, 2001–11

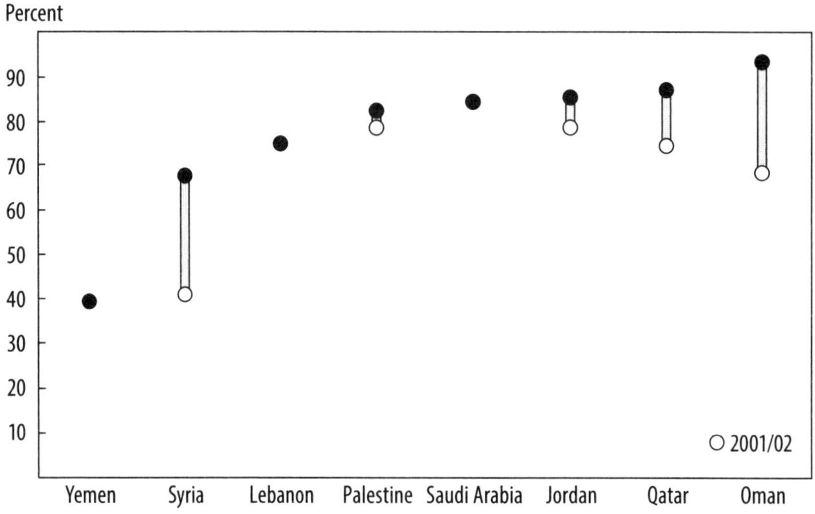

Percent

Source: UNESCO Institute for Statistics database.

while the labor market demands more science, mathematics, and technology graduates. On average, about two-thirds of Arab university graduates major in arts and humanities. This is much higher than in other successful middle-income countries in East Asia and Latin America that tend to put greater emphasis on science and mathematics.[2]

The education literature identifies five skill levels that are usually needed in production processes, each of which requires use of different cognitive skills and decisionmaking capacity. These levels are routine manual tasks that can be described using a set of rules; nonroutine manual tasks that cannot be well described by rules and require optical recognition and fine muscle control; routine cognitive tasks, such as maintaining expense reports, that are well described by logical rules; expert thinking that implies solving problems for which there are no rule-based solutions; and complex communication, which involves interacting with others to obtain and provide information and convince them to take action.[3]

2. See World Bank (2008).
3. See Levy and Murnane (2004).

Recent technical advances have increased the demand for expert thinking and complex communication and decreased demand for other levels of cognitive and decisionmaking capacity.[4] This trend is likely to continue. In response to those changes, education systems around the world have evolved in two directions. First, the configurations of subjects taught at school have changed so that subjects previously reserved for elite education are now more widely available. Second, the kinds of competencies needed have changed with a focus on developing students' transferable skills that would help them adapt to an ever-changing labor market, as well as to living in societies that are continually evolving. In other words, schools need to prepare students for lifelong learning and continuous adaptation to new norms and technologies.

Workers in a twenty-first-century enterprise are increasingly expected to take responsibility and make decisions without turning to hierarchical structures. That is why education reforms around the world have focused on introducing inquiry-based learning and on adapting teaching to the learning capacity of the individual student.

Arab education systems are lagging in this area. Higher-order cognitive skills such as flexibility, problem solving, and judgment are inadequately rewarded in Arab schools, and the individual needs of the students are usually not addressed. Teaching methods remain traditional, with the main activities in Arab schools continuing to be copying from the blackboard, writing, and listening to the teachers. Frontal teaching (wherein a teacher talks to the whole class) is the dominant method. Very little group work, creative thinking, or proactive learning take place.

Moreover, Arab children are not acquiring the basic foundational skills of literacy and numeracy. The 2013 Education for All Global Monitoring Report estimates that 43 percent of children and young people in the Arab region are failing to learn.[5] Steer, Ghanem, and Jalbout (2014) argue, based on the average scores in reading and math for countries for which data were available, that 56 percent of primary school–age children and 48 percent of youth are not learning. By country, this figure ranges from 33 percent of children in Bahrain to 91 percent of children in Yemen who are not learning at the primary level,

4. See Autor, Levy, and Murnane (2003).
5. Education for All Fast-Track Initiative Secretariat (2011).

despite being in school. At the secondary level, more than one-quarter of children are not learning in Lebanon and the United Arab Emirates, while nearly two-thirds are not learning in Morocco.[6]

Now could be the right time to launch an Arab initiative to modernize and strengthen education systems. Arab countries could pool financial and human resources and share knowledge and experience to work together to build world-class education systems. The objective should be to make sure that Arab youth will be able to find decent jobs and be competitive in the twenty-first century and beyond.

Education reform must include changes in curricula as well as in teaching methods. Curricula need to emphasize mathematics, science, and technology. They also need to build competencies—such as problem solving, teamwork, and communication skills—that employers are looking for. This means that teaching methods also need to change from frontal teaching and rote learning to a focus on problem solving and inquiry-based learning. One way to ensure that education reflects the needs of the labor market is to involve the private sector in developing the curricula and in service delivery. This would require the creation of a platform for dialogue and partnership on education between the public and private sectors.

Education reform also needs to include institutional innovations to hold schools and teachers accountable for learning outcomes. It is possible to build on local success stories in the Arab world to develop such innovations. Case studies highlight the importance of accountability relationships and the role of local leadership in building effective parental engagement and improving the quality of service delivery in the education sector. For example, Brixi, Lust, and Woolcock (2015, pp. 3–4) report

In Jordan the Zeid Bin Haritha Secondary School in the village of Yarqa has been achieving excellent results amid poverty and low capacity. Jordan's national School and District Development Program, launched in 2009, encourages schools and directorates to collaborate with parents and communities, and it provides small school grants allowing some autonomy. Involving parents and citizens as partners, however, has not come naturally in traditional communities such as in Yarqa, with its deeply embedded

6. Data from PISA (2009) and TIMMS (2011).

lines of authority. It meant changing the leadership style of the school principal and teachers, creating a sense of common purpose around the school in the community, and establishing new relations through a parent-teacher association and Education Council and making these new structures effective. Significantly, the Education Council in Yarqa has reached out to parents and the wider community and gained their trust for its transparency and inclusive decision making. Furthermore, friendly competition and rivalry among local schools and communities have helped to improve student outcomes. Student performance in national tests has become a source of community prestige and pride.

The experience of Yarqa could inspire similar reforms and institutional innovations across the Arab world.

Agricultural Reforms to End the Exclusion of Smallholder and Family Farmers

Most of the agriculture in the region is under family farming, which is defined as a type of agricultural production system managed by one or more members of a family and primarily reliant on nonwage family labor.[7] Family farming includes agricultural, forestry, fisheries, pastoral, and aquaculture activities. It is often characterized by multiple activities as the family tries to increase its income and diversify its sources to protect itself from exogenous shocks.

Family farmers are often, but not necessarily always, smallholders. However, nearly all smallholders tend to be family farmers. That is why most empirical work on the subject has used the size of landholding as a proxy measure for family farming. Table 6-1 shows the relative importance of small family-run farms (less than five hectares) in Arab countries. On average, about 84 percent of all holdings are under family farming. The importance of family farming appears to be quite uniform across countries. About 55 percent of agricultural landholdings in Algeria and Tunisia are under family farming, as are nearly 70 percent of holdings in Morocco and above 90 percent of holdings in Yemen,

7. See Abaab and others (2000).

TABLE 6-1. Share of Holdings of Less than Five Hectares, Selected Arab Countries
Percent

Country	Share of total holdings	Share of land area
Algeria	55.4	11.3
Egypt	98.2	70.7
Jordan	78.9	23.8
Lebanon	96.7	60.1
Morocco	69.8	23.9
Qatar	73.3	3.4
Tunisia	53.5	10.9
Yemen	93.0	43.9
Average	84.2	25.3

Source: FAO Agriculture Census data. Period covered by country: Algeria, 2001; Egypt, 1999–2000; Morocco, 1996; Jordan, 1997; Lebanon, 1998; Qatar, 2000–01; Tunisia, 2004; Yemen, 2002.

Lebanon, and Egypt. This underlines the importance of family farming for poverty reduction.

Family farms in Arab countries tend to be very small. The average size of a family farm ranges from 0.7 hectare in Egypt to 2.2 hectares in Tunisia. Naturally, it is difficult to make comparisons on the basis of land area alone. For example, 0.7 hectare in the fertile Nile delta may be more productive, and hence worth more, than 2.2 hectares that depend on uncertain rain-fed irrigation in the Tunisian Southwest region.

The second column of table 6-1 shows that while family farms represent the majority of holdings, they control only a small proportion of total agricultural land. About 90 percent of agricultural land in Algeria and Tunisia is under relatively large corporate-type farming. This figure declines to 75 percent in Morocco, 56 percent in Yemen, and 30 percent in Egypt. This reflects the dualistic nature of agriculture in Arab countries, where large numbers of family farms operate alongside big and more modern entities. While family farmers tend to produce for their own consumption (subsistence farming) and to sell to local markets, the large modern farms produce for national and international markets. They tend to have higher productivity and to be more profitable than small family-operated farms. In Morocco, the average large modern farm earns about nine times the earnings of the average family farm. Table 6-2 presents the number of family members working on

TABLE 6-2. Family Farmers as Share of Population, Selected Arab Countries

Country	Smallholders and families working in agriculture (thousands)	Population (thousands)	Ratio of family farmers to population (percent)
Algeria	3,349	36,414	9.2
Egypt	12,647	80,410	15.7
Morocco	3,452	32,245	10.7
Tunisia	489	10,674	4.6

Source: FAO Agriculture Census data. Period covered by country: Algeria, 2001; Egypt, 1999–2000; Morocco, 1996; Tunisia, 2004.

family farms in four Arab countries and their share of the total population. It shows that a large number of people are working on family farms across Arab countries, making family farming a major source of household income and probably the most important source in some countries. About 16 percent of Egypt's population is engaged in family farming. In Morocco and Algeria, nearly 11 percent of the population is engaged in family farming. Even the lower estimate of 4.6 percent of the population in Tunisia is still highly significant.

It is often argued that governments in the region have neglected family farming and focused on the development of large-scale modern agriculture. For example, in Egypt the government invested huge sums in the New Valley (Toshka) project, which aims at irrigating about a quarter of a million hectares of desert land by building a 150-kilometer-long canal from Lake Nasser south of Aswan. Those large projects often have negative social and environmental impacts. On the other hand, it could be argued that developing modern agriculture is a legitimate national objective, as long as it does not come at the expense of family farming.

Morocco's agriculture development program, Plan Maroc Vert, is an example of a strategy that tries to balance the desire to develop modern agriculture with the need to support family farmers. The strategy is built on two pillars: The first aims at developing modern, high-productivity agriculture through large projects built on public-private partnership. The second pillar aims at developing family farming through projects that are mainly government financed. This second pillar consists of 545 projects that, combined, will cost about 20 billion dirhams (US$2.5 billion) over a ten-year period and will target about 950,000 farmers operating in remote and difficult areas. The projects are divided into three types: projects that replace existing crops and products with new ones that provide higher value added to the farmers; projects that enhance productivity of existing products; and projects that introduce new activities to increase family income and diversify its sources. The projects are designed jointly with the professional associations representing the beneficiaries, who are also expected to participate in the project costs (about 30 percent) to ensure ownership and sustainability.

Linking farmers to markets is essential to raising their productivity and standards of living. Raising their share in value added is an important way to improve family farmers' income. Family farmers tend to retain a very small share of value added from their products. For example, a study by the Egyptian Ministry of Agriculture shows that for many vegetables the farmer's share of the market price is only about 20 percent. The absence of marketing, whether domestic or for exports, is a serious constraint on agriculture development and to increasing farmers' incomes. The majority of family farmers in Egypt continue to use the traditional marketing system known as *kerala*. Under this system, the crop is sold in the field at a price per hectare. The buyer takes control of the product in the field and handles the harvesting, selection, grading, and transportation. An obvious problem with this system is that it does not allow for much price differentiation to reflect quality. This also means that the farmer gets a lower share of the market value of the product, as the buyer needs to be compensated for harvesting and grading.

New marketing techniques could be introduced to reduce the role of intermediaries in the marketing process through better organization of family farmers. For example, governments can help promote the products of family farms through special labels and information campaigns about the benefits of consuming local products. Moreover, family farmers' incomes can be raised by establishing links between family farmers and small and medium-size enterprises to process the farmers' products or between family farmers and traders to link farmers with national and international markets. Such links can be created through contract farming or out-grower schemes.

The West Noubaria rural development project in Egypt is an example of a project that helped link smallholder family farmers to the international market. The project helped establish contract farming arrangements

TABLE 6-3. Credit to Agriculture and Credit to the Economy as Shares of GDP,
Selected Arab Countries, 2011

Percent

Country	Credit to agriculture as share of agriculture GDP	Credit to private sector as share of total GDP
Algeria	14.2	30.4
Egypt	7.9	36.8
Mauritania	2.0	29.2
Morocco	7.4	64.9
Tunisia	27.5	54.2

Source: Credit to agriculture and agricultural GDP are from Arab Organization for Agricultural Development, *Statistical Yearbook*, 2012; and credit to the private sector and total GDP are from the Arab Monetary Fund, *Economic Statistics Bulletin*, 2011.

between family farmers producing organic potatoes and an Italian trading company. Thus the farmers were directly linked to the international market and started receiving better prices for their products.[8]

Limited access to financing and investment resources is perhaps the most important constraint facing family farmers. Table 6-3 shows credit to agriculture as a percentage of agricultural GDP and the ratio of credit to the private sector as a percent of total GDP in five countries. It shows that agriculture's share of financing is extremely low compared with its contribution to the economy. In Egypt and Morocco, two large agricultural countries, agriculture's share of credit (adjusted for its contribution to GDP) is less than one-fifth of the average for the whole economy. In Algeria and Tunisia it is about one-half. In Mauritania, agricultural credit is only 2 percent of agricultural GDP.

The data in table 6-3 probably underestimate the magnitude of the problem facing family farmers because a large proportion of agricultural credit goes to big modern farms. Nevertheless, the data confirm that limited access to financing is a major problem for family farmers. Even if one could assume that all the credit to agriculture is going to family farmers, one would still conclude that they are grossly underserved by the financial system compared with other sectors of the economy.

Existing financial institutions, credit instruments, and bank procedures are ill adapted to the needs of family farmers. Farmers are not

8. See Ghanem (2014b).

able to provide the kind of guarantees that banks require to lend, since many family farmers do not have notarized land titles. The amounts of credit required by individual family farmers are usually small and are not of interest to banks. Moreover, many banks consider agriculture to be too risky and prefer not to lend to it.

To deal with this situation governments may consider creating new institutions or reinforcing existing ones with simplified lending procedures that are adapted to the realities of family farmers; putting in place lines of credit to encourage banks to lend to family farmers; developing insurance and guarantee facilities to reduce the risk of lending to agriculture; and encouraging the development and expansion of rural microcredit facilities as well as farmer-centered financial institutions (where farmers have a stake in these institutions). There is also a need to increase public investment in agriculture and in rural areas to build the social and physical infrastructure necessary for the development of family farming.

There are several examples from Arab countries of initiatives to enhance financing for smallholders and family farmers. Sudan created a Micro Finance Development Facility owned by the Central Bank and the Ministry of Finance and mainly funded from donor resources. It has supported the creation of sixteen new microfinance institutions and has reached nearly half a million beneficiaries. About 80 percent of funding under this program is directed to agriculture activities. The facility funds small investments by family farmers and gives special preference to women and young graduates from agriculture and veterinary colleges.

Lebanon's Disaster Fund for Agriculture is an example of an initiative to provide guarantees and reduce the riskiness of family farming. Half of the resources for this fund are provided by the government and the other half by the farmers themselves. The idea is to provide financial compensation to farmers suffering from bad weather conditions or other types of natural disasters. By reducing farmers' risks, this fund also helps them obtain credit.

Access to land is another important issue for smallholder family farmers. As suggested earlier, the average size of a family farm in Arab countries is less than two hectares. Moreover, this average size is decreasing steadily as a result of population increase. The application of inheritance laws that divide land among surviving children and the absence of well-functioning land markets that allow consolidation compound the problem. The small size of family farms complicates their access to technology, inputs, and markets.

Many family farmers in Arab countries do not have title to their small holdings. In some countries, land continues to be legally owned by the state, and farmers are considered tenants, although they often lack a legal document proving this relationship. In addition to making it difficult for family farmers to obtain credit, uncertainty about their ownership of land discourages them from investing. Governments could help boost investment in agriculture by facilitating land titling for farmers and in some cases distributing public and collective land to smallholder family farmers. It is also recommended that laws and regulations be amended to protect the rights of tenants on small farms.

Research and extension services should be adapted to the needs of family farmers. Productivity of Arab countries' family farmers is lagging partly because of lack of access to appropriate modern technology. Regional institutions need to carry out their own agricultural research to adapt existing knowledge and techniques to local ecological, social, and economic realities. Many studies show that the return to investment in agricultural research is typically very high, and it is estimated at 36 percent for Arab countries. However, as is shown in figure 6-3, Arab countries' investment in research ranges from 0.4 to 0.9 percent of agricultural GDP, far below the rate of about 2.4 percent observed in the Organization for Economic Cooperation and Development (OECD) countries and the 1.5 percent observed in successful Latin American countries.

Perhaps more important, many extension services in Arab countries are poorly funded and therefore ineffective. Moreover, extension workers are often not trained to communicate with family farmers and end up delivering information in a manner that is not convincing or helpful to the farmers. This appears to be a problem across the Arab world. For example, a recent study in Jordan compared productivity of olive farmers who received support from extension services with those who received no support.[9] The study concluded that receiving support from extension services had no impact on productivity. This implies that even when research is carried out successfully, its results are not

9. See al-Sharafat, Altarawaneh, and Altahat (2012).

FIGURE 6-3. Investment in Agricultural Research as Share of Agricultural GDP, Selected Countries, 2008

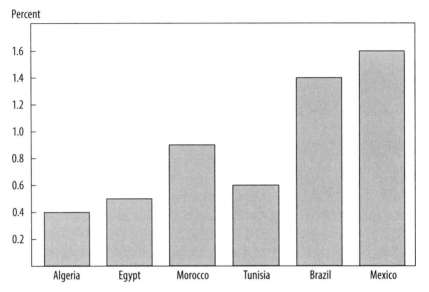

Source: World Bank, FAO, and International Fund for Agricultural Development (2009).

adequately transmitted to smallholder family farmers. It appears that there is a need to consider innovative types of research and extension institutions as well as new instruments for delivering information to family farmers. Innovative extension systems put family farmers at the center and do not consider them as mere end receivers. New institutions could be based on government partnerships with the private sector, family-farmer-producer organizations, and civil society. Many civil society organizations have earned the trust of family farmers because they have deep knowledge of the sector and long experience working with family farmers. They increasingly use modern technologies and information technologies such as mobile phones and the Internet to deliver information to family farmers. The use of dedicated television programs to provide information to farmers in Egypt is an interesting example in this area.

Better research and extension services are particularly needed to help family farmers adapt to the impact of climate change. Higher tempera-tures, less rainfall, and increased land salinity (which are predicted to result from climate change) in a region that is already very hot and arid and in which per capita water availability is among the lowest in the world do not augur well for the future of agriculture in the region, unless urgent action is taken now. Family farmers should be at the center of action to adapt to climate change. They are the largest producers of food for local consumption and creators of rural employment, and at the same time their small size and lack of investment resources make them particularly vulnerable to climate change and other types of shocks.

Some farmers are already adapting to higher temperatures by adjusting planting times. Research and extension services can be helpful here by introducing new varieties that are more heat resistant and by informing farmers about new cropping patterns to reflect changes in climatic conditions. Arab countries' biggest challenge will continue to be dealing with water shortages. Here again, research and extension can play an important role by introducing more drought-resistant varieties. This needs to be accompanied by new investments in better irrigation systems to avoid water waste and ensure the most efficient use of limited water resources.

In addition to better policies and programs, promoting agriculture and supporting smallholder family farmers require new and more inclusive institutions. Producer organizations and cooperatives can play an important role in strengthening the governance system of the agriculture sector, particularly in developing and supporting family farmers and therefore in increasing the productivity of this sector. Problems caused by the large number of very small dispersed family farms in Arab countries can be tackled through the development of strong producer organizations that group farmers together to ensure that their voice is heard in policy discussions and also help enhance access to technology, input and output markets, information, communication, and natural resources. Compared with other regions with similar per capita income (for example, Latin America or East Asia), producer organizations, as well as other civic society organizations that operate in rural areas, are still quite weak in the Arab countries and do not yet fully play their roles in supporting family farming.

Arab countries are characterized by a multiplicity of weak producer organizations that are highly dependent on governments. In several countries the statutes place producers and other civil society organizations under the administrative supervision and authority of the government. Thus their autonomy and ability to operate in support of family farmers is restricted. Moreover, producer organizations are usually heavily dependent on government budgets for financial support, which further erodes their independence and limits their areas of action. In fact, producer organizations sometimes act more as government agencies, informing farmers of policy decisions that are taken at the central level and helping implement them, rather than as bodies that represent farmers and advocate for policies that protect their interests.

Many producer organizations suffer from inadequate human, financial, and material resources, which severely limits their ability to participate in agricultural and rural development. Lack of training and knowledge among grassroots actors limits the organizations' ability to identify issues and mobilize appropriate expertise at different levels to deal with them. Moreover, lack of members with experience and training negatively affects the way collective and individual responsibilities are being exercised in various producer organizations.

Family farmers need effective producer organizations and cooperatives. Those organizations should play an important political role. Family farmers do not feel that their voices are being heard in policy circles. The lack of strength and the low level of political participation of organizations that represent family farmers may explain why development strategies and policies tend to be biased in favor of urban activities and large modern agriculture. Independent and strong producer organizations could play an effective advocacy role and could help lobby politicians to promote the interests of family farmers.

Producer organizations and cooperatives should also play an important economic role, grouping family farmers together to enhance their access to technology and inputs, improve market access, and help them retain a larger share of value added. Producer organizations could encourage the exchange of experience and know-how between farmers. They could propose and encourage programs for applied agricultural research that support family farmers and also help improve extension services and adapt them to the needs of family farmers. In fact, civil society organizations, including producer organizations and cooperatives, are often much better placed than government agencies to deliver extension and technical support to family farmers.

When provided with adequate support, family farmers are able to meet quality standards and sell for export, thus considerably increasing their incomes. Some civil society organizations have been active in this area with good results. The SUN (*al-shamas* in Arabic) nongovern-mental organization, which was created in 2002 and operates in Upper Egypt, is a good example.[10] This organization works with family farmers in one of the poorest regions in Egypt. It supports the creation of asso-ciations and provides them with technical, managerial, and marketing support. It helps link family farmers to large producers and exporters through different contractual arrangements and out-grower schemes. In its first five years of operation, it signed nearly 900 different contracts with exporters and agro-processors. It also prioritizes women's partic-ipation in the program. By 2007 more than 12,500 family farmers had joined SUN associations. They exported nontraditional products worth 85 million Egyptian pounds (about US$12 million) and estimate that participants' income rose by 60 million pounds (about US$8 million).

Producer organizations and cooperatives can also work across national borders and therefore help in regional integration, in addition to supporting family farmers. The Union of Sheep and Goat Growers Associations in the Maghreb is a good example in this area. The union was created in 2011 by growers associations in Morocco, Algeria, Tuni-sia, and Mauritania. Its overarching objective is to set up a regional professional framework for organizations of sheep and goat growers so as to contribute to the development of the subsector in the countries of the Maghreb. It facilitates knowledge sharing across the subregion and works to elaborate joint strategies and programs as well as joint coor-dination mechanisms among its member organizations. This growers association also operates as an advocacy group to defend the interests of its membership. As a union of several national producer organiza-tions it has more political weight than any of its individual members and hence can be a more effective interlocutor with governments.

Governments need to support producer organizations, cooperatives, and other civil society organizations working with family farmers and to ensure their political and financial independence. This may require an enabling environment that would entail legal and policy changes that provide more autonomy to civil society organizations, moves them out of governments' control, and provides them with greater financial and operational freedom. It will also require a change in the current bureaucratic and political culture away from centralized control and

10. Ministry of Agriculture and Land Reclamation (2009), box 4, p. 59.

toward a much more decentralized and participatory system of governance. Governments should regularly invite producer organizations and cooperatives' representatives to participate as equal partners in the formulation and implementation of policies and development programs.

Women and Economic Empowerment

The Arab Spring opened up a prospect of opportunity for women. Like their male counterparts, young women demanded an inclusive role in society, economic growth, and access to employment opportunities. The demographic shift toward youth population has brought young women to the forefront. This new generation of women aged fifteen to twenty-nine is more educated and has better health outcomes and lower fertility rates than its predecessors. Still, the labor force participation rate for young Arab women is particularly low compared with the rest of the world. It stood at about 27 percent, on average, in 2003 (see figure 6-4) compared with 64 percent in the Americas, 55 percent in Europe, and 62 percent in sub-Saharan Africa.

Social and cultural norms, legal and regulatory frameworks, and economic factors are all responsible for creating gender disparity in labor force participation. In the Middle East and North Africa (MENA) region, gender norms are defined by the patriarchal system. According to Offenhauer (2005, p. 10), the patriarchal system in Muslim societies is characterized by "male domination, early marriage, son preference, restrictive codes of behavior for women, and the association of family honor with female virtue." It can be argued that these gender norms translate into cultural and social norms and restrict women's access to the labor market.

On the other hand, the recent wave of the World Values Survey (2010–14) shows that women do care about education and jobs. Figure 6-5 shows that across the MENA region, women consider education and employment as important priorities for themselves. More than 40 percent of women in Lebanon and Morocco disagree with the priority given to men in jobs. In eight of the sampled countries, more than 60 percent of women agree with the importance of having a job for independence, and in Jordan, Libya, Morocco, Palestine, and Tunisia more than 40 percent of women strongly disagree with the notion that a university education is more important for a boy than for a girl.

FIGURE 6-4. Female and Male Labor Force Participation across MENA, Aged Fifteen to Sixty-Four, Selected Arab Countries, Various Years

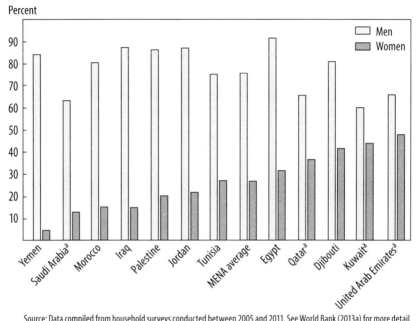

Source: Data compiled from household surveys conducted between 2005 and 2011. See World Bank (2013a) for more detail.
a. Official estimates for national nonimmigrant population.

The Arab world has a very high level of legal restriction on women, which could explain the low female labor force participation rate. For example, a husband's unilateral right of divorce and a wife's legal obligation to obey her husband may create an additional barrier to women's entry into the labor force. On the other hand, Morikawa (2015b) notes that many Arab countries have laws that prohibit labor discrimination in the workplace. Hence the low level of female labor force participation often stems from de facto discrimination rather than from de jure discrimination.

This seems to be especially applicable to Morocco. Morikawa (2015b) presents a social institution and gender index by considering a country's family code, civil liberties, the physical integrity of citizens, traditional preferences for male offspring, and ownership rights. Morocco is ranked forty-third among more than 100 non-OECD countries, the second-highest ranking for an Arab country after Tunisia. In fact, significant reforms to the Moroccan family law, Moudawana, in 2004 led to a

FIGURE 6-5. Women's Voice in Selected Arab Countries, 2011–13[a]

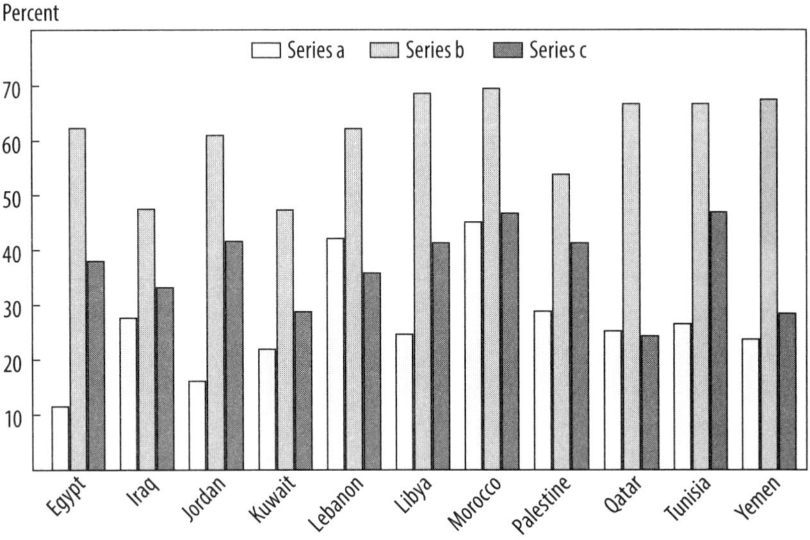

Percent

Source: World Values Survey, wave 6, 2010–14. Period covered by country: Egypt, 2012; Iraq, 2013; Jordan, 2014; Kuwait, 2013; Lebanon, 2013; Libya, 2013; Morocco, 2011; Palestinian Territories, 2013; Qatar, 2010; Tunisia, 2013; Yemen 2013.

a. Series a = Proportion of women who disagree with the statement "When jobs are scarce, men should have more right to a job than women." Series b = Proportion of women who agree with the statement "Having a job is the best way for a women to be an independent person." Series c = Proportion of women who strongly disagree with the statement "A university education is more important for a boy than a girl."

rise in the minimum marriage age for women from fifteen to eighteen, placed a family under the joint responsibility of both spouses, and eliminated a woman's legal obligation to obey her husband. However, there remain issues regarding enforcement, as some judges have circumvented the law, while others are still unfamiliar with the amendments. In 2012 roughly 10 percent of the marriages recorded in Morocco involved a girl under the age of eighteen, permitted under articles 20 and 21 of Moudawana, which allow family judges to authorize the marriage of minors. Even though the articles require well-substantiated arguments to justify such marriages, more than 90 percent of requests are authorized. By removing legal restrictions on women, including those that are implicit, the society would be better prepared for working women.[11]

Added to the gender norms and social and institutional constraints, economic conditions have also hampered employment opportunities

11. For more on the case of Morocco, see Morikawa (2015b).

FIGURE 6-6. Ratio of Female to Male Primary Enrollment, Selected Arab Countries, 2000 and 2010

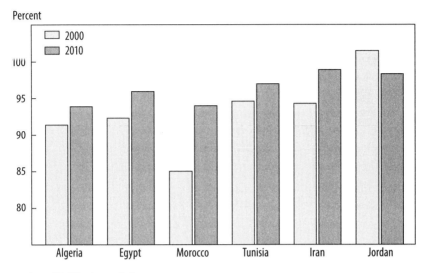

Source: World Development Indicators.

for women. As employment in the public sector fell, and the under-developed private sector could not absorb the unmet demand for employment, the informal sector grew. Most young Arabs get their first job in the informal sector.[12] However, Arab women shy away from the informal sector owing to its insecure working conditions. While both men and women aspire to public sector jobs, women consider government jobs more "acceptable, personally and socially."[13] In addition, the connections and networks required to get jobs in the increasingly shrinking public sector give preference to men. The World Bank (2013a) report highlights the prevalence of a gender bias in women's access to job-relevant skills and entrepreneurship opportunities among factors that reduce female labor force participation.

Surprisingly, there appears to be little gender bias in access to education. Arab countries have done particularly well in improving the ratio of female to male school enrollment. Figures 6-6 and 6-7 show that the gender gap in enrollment at the primary and secondary levels decreased

12. See Devarajan and Mottaghi (2015).
13. World Bank (2013a, p. 98).

FIGURE 6-7. Ratio of Female to Male Secondary Enrollment, Selected Arab Countries, 2000 and 2010

Percent

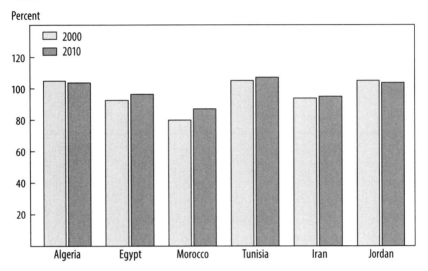

Source: World Development Indicators.

from 2000 to 2010. The ratio of female to male primary school enroll-ment has gone up close to or above 95 percent in all six countries. The secondary enrollment ratio has also improved for Egypt, Morocco, and Tunisia while remaining stagnant at above 100 percent for Jordan and Algeria.

The learning crisis is affecting boys much more than girls. The per-centage of girls who meet basic learning levels is higher than that for boys in all nine Arab states for which learning data are available. At the primary level, Saudi Arabia shows the largest disparity, with nearly half of the boys not learning but fewer than one-third of the girls not learning.

Girls also learn more than boys while in secondary school. In nine of the eleven Arab states for which learning outcomes are available, higher proportions of girls are learning than boys. In four countries, Bahrain, Jordan, Oman, and the United Arab Emirates, the share of boys not learning was at least 15 percentage points higher than the share of girls not learning (see figure 6-8).[14]

14. See Steer, Ghanem and Jalbout (2014).

FIGURE 6-8. Fifteen-Year-Old Girls and Boys Not Meeting Basic Learning Level, Selected Arab Countries, 2009 and 2011

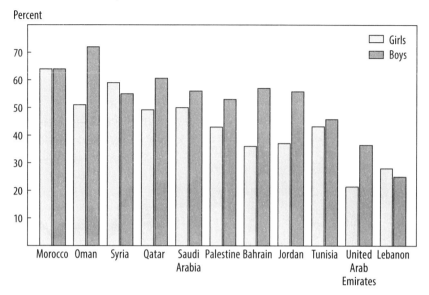

Source: Data from PISA (2009), and TIMMS (2011). Author's calculations.

Even if women are better educated overall, their economic activity remains weak, and their unemployment rate is systematically higher than men's.[15] The case of Jordan is fairly typical of Arab countries. Women represent less than 20 percent of the labor force, and a smaller share of Jordanian women work (less than 16 percent). That is, women are largely excluded from the economic and productive process. Women's activity rate by age suggests that until women are in their late twenties, their participation increases, but contrary to men it decreases from then on (see figure 6-9). The contrast is striking since almost all men between the ages of twenty-five and forty are part of the workforce. It means that from the beginning of their work lives, women lag men in the job market, in terms of experience and date of entry.

Participation dramatically increases for women with diplomas (in 2012 less than 6 percent of women with no more than a secondary education participated in the workforce, 31 percent with an intermediate diploma, and 57 percent with at least a bachelor's degree); for

15. See Amer (2012).

FIGURE 6-9. Employment Activity, by Sex and Age, Jordan, 2013

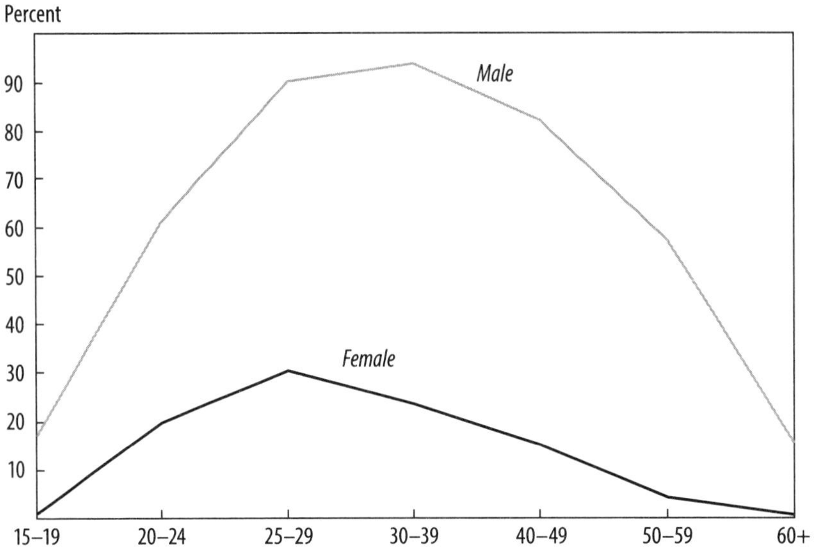

Percent

Source: Department of Statistics, Jordan.

men, the added value of an intermediate diploma or higher degree is important, but even illiterate men participate in the workforce at more than 20 percent (table 6-4). Assaad, Hendy, and Yassine (2012) argue that the ability of educated women to get a job in the government, and in the private sector to a lesser extent, is the reason for the discrepancy between education levels. However, women's unemployment rate rises systemically with education, more strongly than for men (for whom the correlation is weaker).

Marriage seems to push women to drop out of the workforce (the opposite is true for men).[16] Whatever the level of education, married woman are indeed less present in the labor force. This is particularly true for women with higher education: half of the married women are out of the labor market, while that is the case for only 21 percent of unmarried women. This pattern holds true to a lesser extend for women with secondary degrees, while the difference for less educated women is marginal. Moreover, it can be noted that the group of women

16. And childbearing, most probably.

TABLE 6-4. Economic Activity, by Sex and Education Level, Jordan, 2012

Percent

Sex and education level	Percentage	Economically active			Not eco-nomically active	Unemploy-ment rate
		Total	Employed	Unemployed		
Total		38.0	33.4	4.6	62.0	12.2
Illiterate	100	6.8	6.2	0.6	93.2	9.3
Less than secondary	100	34.8	30.9	3.9	65.2	11.2
Secondary	100	25.4	23.2	2.2	74.6	8.6
Intermediate	100	50.7	45.2	5.5	49.3	10.8
Bachelor and above	100	70.8	59.6	11.2	29.2	15.9
Men						
Total		61.3	54.9	6.4	38.7	10.4
Illiterate	100	21.9	19.6	2.3	78.1	10.4
Less than secondary	100	60.4	53.6	6.8	39.6	11.2
Secondary	100	45.2	41.4	3.7	54.8	8.3
Intermediate	100	80.3	74.9	5.4	19.7	6.8
Bachelor and above	100	82.6	73.5	9.1	17.4	11
Women						
Total		14.1	11.3	2.8	85.9	19.9
Illiterate	100	1.3	1.3	0	98.7	2.1
Less than secondary	100	3.8	3.4	0.4	96.2	11.0
Secondary	100	5.6	5.0	0.6	94.4	11.0
Intermediate	100	30.9	25.4	5.5	69.1	17.8
Bachelor and above	100	57.1	43.4	13.7	42.9	24.0

Source: Assaad, Hendy, and Yassine (2012).

with the highest unemployment rate is unmarried educated women, 26 percent of whom are unemployed.[17]

Teaching is the main economic activity for women (more than 40 percent of the active women are in the education sector) (table 6-5). The health sector and public administration follow (less than 15 percent in 2012), which illustrates the fact that outside of the public sector, women are present in few economic activities.

17. Assaad, Hendy, and Yassine (2012, tables 1 and 2, p. 27).

TABLE 6-5.   Top Ten Economic Activities for Working-Age Women, Jordan, 2012

Percent

Activity	Kingdom	Rural	Urban
Education	41.8	47.9	40.6
Human health and social work activities	14.3	15.4	14.1
Public administration and defense; compulsory social security	12.1	17.7	11.1
Manufacturing	6.4	5.9	6.5
Wholesale and retail trade; repair of motor vehicles and motorcycles	5.5	3.4	5.9
Financial and insurance activities	3.2	0.7	3.6
Professional, scientific, and technical activities	3.0	0.9	3.4
Other service activities	2.8	1.6	3.1
Activities of households as employers; undifferentiated goods- and services-producing activities of households for own use	2.5	0.6	2.8
Information and communication	1.9	0.4	2.2

Source: Department of Statistics, Employment and Unemployment Survey, Jordan.

Assaad, Hendy, and Yassine (2012) use the panel data gathered in 2010 to study the dynamics of women's employment over the past forty years. They find that among women, "new entrants were much more reliant on government jobs in the 1970s and 1980s than their men counterparts."[18] The rate of female employment in the government sector was higher than 60 percent until 1985; it then fell to 25 percent in the late 1990s and rose to 30 percent in the first decade of this century. The slowdown in government jobs first affected women, as men continued to be hired in high numbers until the late 1990s. The job status of women subsequently became more precarious in both the informal wage sector and in temporary private employment. Studying the trajectories of young women entering the labor market, the authors confirm that many women drop out of the workforce in the first ten years, especially from less family-friendly jobs (that is, outside of government). The only mobility appears to be from formal private jobs to government jobs.

The above discussion indicates that the problem of female economic inclusion and labor force participation is complex and multifaceted.

18. See Assaad, Hendy, and Yassine (2012, p. 6).

TABLE 6-6. Family Workers on Family Farms, by Sex, Selected Arab Countries

Country	Male workers	Female workers (thousands)	Total (thousands)	Share of women (percent)
Algeria	2,580	769	3,349	23.0
Egypt	8,227	4,420	12,647	34.9
Tunisia	334	155	489	31.7
Yemen	2,105	1,344	3,449	38.9

Source: FAO, Agriculture Census data. Period covered for country: Algeria, 2001; Egypt, 1999–2000; Tunisia, 2004; Yemen, 2002.

Improving the economic status of women in the Arab world would require action in at least three areas. First, the legal and regulatory frameworks would need to be revised to abolish discrimination against women, and at the same time institutions will need to be strengthened to ensure that the new rules are actually implemented and the discrimination is effectively removed. Second, policies and programs to expand the formal private sector would help increase the supply of decent jobs that are considered safe for women. Third, a continued expansion of female access to quality education will increase overall labor force participation rates, since there is a positive correlation between a woman's level of education and her decision to enter the job market.

Special attention needs to be paid to women in agriculture. Women play an important role in family farming. Table 6-6 presents the distribution of family farm workers by sex in four countries. It shows that between 23 and 39 percent of the labor on family farms is provided by women. Moreover, the role of women in family farming is increasing because more and more male family members are migrating to oil-rich countries and to cities to earn a better living and send remittances to their families, who remain on the farm. Women are left to look after the family farm. As a result, a process of feminization of family farming in Arab countries seems to have started.

There is a common division of labor between men and women on the family farm. Women tend to be responsible for food production and for animal husbandry. They plant food crops for their families' consumption, and they look after small and large ruminants and specialize in the production of eggs, milk, and dairy products. They also participate with all family members in harvesting activities. They are usually helped by their children, who take small ruminants to water and pasture and work alongside their parents at harvest time.

Women farmers suffer from lack of access to land, credit, and technology. Women landholders generally represent less than 5 percent of landholders in the region. Moreover, the small size of farms and land fragmentation pose a special problem for women, who are hampered by social norms from moving among plots that may be far from one another. Women have great difficulties in obtaining rural credit. The husbands' agreement is often required, which may not always be forthcoming. There is also the requirement of literacy to sign legally binding documents. Older women, who participate most in commercial activities and can benefit readily from microcredit, are the least likely to be literate. Women often have to form associations to obtain microcredit. These organizational requirements can be time consuming and often require the presence of an agent in the community.

Rural women have little access to extension services. Most extension programs lack qualified personnel and have limited capacity to mainstream gender in policies, programs, and implementation strategies. The design of many extension programs has not taken women's cultural and time constraints into account. Consequently, women's opportunities to express their needs and to have them met are more limited than those of men. Research and extension work tend to focus on cash crops rather than the subsistence food crops that women grow on land they own. Although women play a predominant role in all forms of animal husbandry, including raising small ruminants, caring for cows, and preparing all milk products, extension services for women rarely focus on those activities.

Given their important role in agriculture and in food and nutrition security, particular attention needs to be paid to the needs of women farmers.[19] Governments could consider a three-pronged approach to supporting women farmers. First, existing laws on access to land and to credit need to be reviewed and, whenever appropriate, revised to remove biases against women farmers. In addition, many existing procedures, particularly those regulating titling land as well as obtaining microfinance, need to be revised and simplified to reflect the realities of rural women. Second, governments could put in place special programs

19. See Food and Agriculture Organization (2011).

to provide financial services for rural women, such as an agricultural women's bank that would specialize in working with women farmers and catering to their banking needs. Third, extension services and programs need to be revised to better reflect the increased feminization of family farming. For example, Sudan has developed Woman Farmer Schools, a program that caters to the needs of rural women and shares information on health and nutrition issues as well as on agricultural production and animal husbandry.

7

How Can the International Community Help?

The international community is interested in inclusive growth in the Arab world because it would contribute to peace and stability. And peace and stability in the Arab world are global public goods. Instability in the Arab region spills over to the rest of the world through refugees, illegal migration, and, of course, terrorism.

Many analysts, for example, Wittes (2008), go a step further and argue that it is in the interest of the international community, and particularly the United States, to promote democracy in the Arab world. The rise in violence and extremism is viewed as a reaction to the lack of democratic governance. Hence those analysts call for an active policy of supporting democratization to contribute to peace and stability. Of course, democracy and human rights also impact economic development, and there is a growing literature on the role of human rights in development.[1]

But can the international community really influence short-term political developments in the region? Probably not. Nevertheless, it is important that the international community remain engaged in the region. However, it may also be necessary to reexamine the nature of this engagement and reorient aid flows toward areas and sectors that directly enhance economic and political inclusiveness. Examples of such areas would be institution building, support for small-scale enterprises, agriculture and rural development, and education.[2]

---

1. For example, see World Bank and OECD (2013).
2. This chapter is based on the analysis in Ghanem and Shaikh (2013).

Adopting a Long-Term View: Can the West Be Patient?

Achieving the goal of a stable democracy requires peace. It also requires building important institutions (such as a free press, independent judiciary, political parties, and so on) that ensure transparency, voice, and accountability. Most important, it requires a change of political culture toward greater inclusion and acceptance of the other. Those changes take years to materialize. Therefore, patience and a long-term vision are needed. International aid could be used strategically and be combined with knowledge sharing and technology transfer to influence the path of the transition and help achieve greater inclusion and social justice.

Economic support to the region could focus on fixing the problems with the growth model adopted before the Arab Spring. It could tackle questions of social justice and inclusiveness. Achieving inclusive growth that is associated with the development of institutions that provide for transparency, voice, and accountability in decisionmaking, an expansion of the middle class, and the growth of small businesses would be important for the democratization process. International economic support for the region could prioritize inclusiveness and social justice by supporting institutional development, helping small businesses, and investing in agriculture, rural development, and education.

Developing Inclusive Economic Institutions: How Can Donors Overcome Political Sensitivities?

Inclusive institutions are important for democracy, and they are important for social justice. Most Arab governments over the past four decades have at least given lip service to the goal of social justice and have taken some symbolic steps toward implementing parts of this agenda. However, there has been no serious attempt made so far to fully implement an agenda for achieving social justice and economic inclusion. Even after the revolutions, transition governments did not take any significant moves toward achieving this key goal.

Arab governments' failure to act decisively on social justice issues could be explained by the fact that the lower middle class and the poor who would benefit from such an agenda have little or no voice in the economic decisionmaking process. This could explain why their interests were not served by economic policies, while a system of crony capitalism flourished. Inclusive economic institutions that would give voice to ordinary citizens in economic policymaking and empower them to hold government officials accountable would increase the probability that an agenda for achieving social justice is actually adopted and implemented. It would provide important support for the democratization efforts.

The allocation of public investment is often biased toward relatively better-off regions and groups, which reflects the noninclusive nature of the planning and economic decisionmaking process. Sakamoto (2013) analyzes Egypt's planning system and finds that lack of a structured dialogue among key stakeholders is a key feature of the planning process in Egypt. Six five-year development plans were prepared during the Mubarak era. Budget allocations were determined before determining economic goals and strategies. The first planning step was the production of the investment budget allocation sheet by the Ministry of Planning, based on the line ministries' investment budget requests. The five-year development plan was then drafted by the Ministry of Planning based on the budget allocation sheet. This system was simple, with drafting being fully completed inside the Ministry of Planning without official outside contacts. Thus the system excluded major stakeholders, such as the private sector, civil society organizations, labor organizations, and farmer organizations. Even line ministries had little voice in the preparation of the plan document.

Kharas and Abdou (2012) look at the role that civil society organizations could play in achieving inclusive growth and social justice. They argue that such organizations can make four important contributions to inclusive growth. First, they can play an advocacy role for small businesses, the informal sector, and other marginalized groups, ensuring that government takes their concerns into account when formulating policies and programs. And they can also act as whistleblowers, denouncing corruption and other unfair practices that harm small or weak economic agents. Second, they could provide important economic services that the public sector is unable to provide (or provides inefficiently): for example, by helping small enterprises get access to finance and to technical assistance. Third, they can act as think tanks, developing ideas and promoting best practices that support inclusive growth. Fourth, they can be an important source of employment opportunities for youth. Kharas and Abdou (2012) conclude that the legal framework governing civil society organizations needs to be reformed to provide them with greater flexibility and incentives to expand their activities.

Farmer organizations and cooperatives are a special type of civil society organization that can play an important role in strengthening the governance system of the agriculture sector, particularly in developing and supporting family farmers. Problems caused by the large number of family farms with very small holdings can be tackled through the development of strong producer organizations that group farmers together to ensure that their voice is heard in policy discussions and also help enhance access to technology, inputs, and markets. Existing farmer organizations and cooperatives are weak and are overly dependent on government for financial and technical support, which erodes their independence and limits their areas of action. Cooperatives and farmer organizations sometimes act more as government agencies, informing farmers of policy decisions that are taken at the central level and helping implement them, rather than as bodies that represent farmers and advocate for policies that protect their interests.

These are just three examples of areas where support for institution building is badly needed. International support to institution building could be a sensitive subject as it may raise political issues. Experience with U.S. funding for Egyptian civil society organizations is an example of how things can go wrong.[3] But this should not be an argument for doing nothing. Instead, it should be an argument for engaging the governments of the region in a serious dialogue on the issue. Inclusiveness and social justice cannot be achieved without institutions that ensure transparency of decisionmaking, provide voice to all stakeholders, and hold government officials accountable.[4]

Some members of the international community are particularly well equipped to provide support to the development of inclusive economic institutions. The United Nations Development Program, which has a strong presence in the region, has a clear mandate in the area of human rights that includes the principles of transparency, voice, and accountability. Moreover, it is a neutral UN agency that can provide needed

3. Egyptian authorities closed down a number of U.S.-supported NGOs and started legal proceedings against their staff on the grounds that they were not registered and were illegally receiving funding from abroad.

4. For more on the role of institutions in development, see Acemoglu and Robinson (2012).

support to nongovernmental organizations, legislatures, and the free press without necessarily being accused of political meddling. Another UN agency, the Food and Agriculture Organization, has a long experience of working with farmer organizations. The International Monetary Fund and the World Bank have vast experience in the area of public financial management, procurement policies, and civil service reforms. The Japan International Cooperation Agency has experience in the area of inclusive planning. The European Commission, Canada, and the United Kingdom have experience in supporting organizations that promote transparency, voice, and accountability, including in the Arab world.

Supporting Small Business: Could Donors Move beyond Simple Credit Programs?

The expansion of the small and medium-size enterprise sector would help promote economic inclusiveness as it would provide greater opportunities especially for youth. It would also contribute to a gradual democratic transition. When the private sector consists of a small number of large firms they tend to build special links to government. Those connected firms are happy to support autocratic regimes that provide them with protection and other privileges such as access to financing, government contracts, and public infrastructure. Thus a system of autocracy and crony capitalism grows and tends to perpetuate itself. The owners of large businesses have no interest in promoting democracy, as it could disrupt their special relations with government. In his study of Egypt, Rutherford (2008) argues that autocracy can be countered by supporting a large number of small business owners who would normally exert pressure to institute legal and institutional reforms that would level the playing field and break the link between powerful capitalists and autocratic governments. They would also call for democratic reforms so as to use electoral politics to push for policy reforms to support small businesses.

Most donors have programs to support small and medium-size enterprises and youth entrepreneurship, and they need to be refined and scaled up. In addition to providing access to financing, those programs need to prioritize technology transfer and market access. Vocational and entrepreneurship training programs are also important to correct some of the weaknesses of the Arab education system. Successful programs for the development of small and medium-size enterprises are usually based on partnership between governments (that provide funding), civil society organizations (that provide training), and the organized private sector (that provides technology and markets). In the case of most Arab countries, those partnerships still need to be developed. In particular, donors can help connect domestic small and medium-size enterprises with foreign investors and export markets.

Access to regional and international markets is important for business development and job creation. The international community could make a huge contribution to the development of exports and job creation. It could facilitate exports of manufactured goods from Arab countries, especially for mechanical and electrical industries and construction materials, by negotiating mutual recognition agreements to reduce technical barriers to trade. Agriculture and agro-processing is an important sector for many Arab countries (for example, Morocco, Tunisia, and Egypt), and it is also a sector where small and medium-size enterprises could easily develop. The international community could improve Arab countries' access to agricultural markets by removing nontariff barriers to agricultural trade. This would require, among other things, the abolition of quotas, reference prices, and seasonal restrictions, especially for exports of fruits and vegetables.[5]

Support to Backward Regions and the Rural Poor: Is It Possible to End Decades of Neglect?

A strategy to achieve inclusive growth will have to deal with the problems of regional inequalities and rural poverty. For many years no real action has been taken to develop backward regions or support the rural poor. This had serious political consequences as some backward regions became centers of extremism and sometimes even violence. It also had serious social and economic consequences. Illiteracy, child malnutrition, and even stunting continue to be unacceptably high in rural areas, particularly in Upper Egypt. Intervention is needed in two

5. For more on the importance of opening up developed country markets to Arab country exports, see Chauffour (2013).

areas: social protection for the rural poor and development of agriculture and agro-industries.

In most Arab countries, social protection has been provided to the populations of large cities through a system of untargeted price subsidies. In the rural areas, social protection is usually project based and therefore fragmented. There is a need to move to a systems-based approach to social protection. Arabs can benefit from Latin America's experience in this area, especially Brazil's Bolsa Familia and Mexico's Progresa-Oportunidades. This experience shows that direct cash transfers can be used to achieve poverty reduction as well as development objectives. By providing cash to poor families those programs help raise their consumption and get them out of poverty. It is a much more direct method than generalized price subsidies for products that can be consumed by the poor as well as the nonpoor. By making part of the transfer conditional on school attendance or immunization the programs also encourage investment in human capital and thus help achieve long-term development objectives. There is also some evidence that recipients of cash transfers in rural areas tend to save part of it and use it for investments in productive physical capital.

Agriculture is crucial for many Arab economies and particularly for poor households. All of the poor in rural areas are either directly or indirectly affected by agriculture. Therefore, agriculture growth and the resulting growth in the nonfarm rural economy would have significant poverty-reducing effects. It would also have strong equalization effects as it reduces the large income gaps between urban and rural areas.

The international community has a great deal of experience in social protection and agriculture development and could provide important support to achieving inclusive growth through financing and knowledge sharing. The World Bank has done extensive work on social safety nets and can support reforms in this area. Several donors are funding agriculture development, and UN agencies (mostly the Food and Agriculture Organization) are providing technical assistance and knowledge sharing. They could scale up their interventions and focus them on supporting smallholder farmers, particularly in the poorest areas.

References

Abaab, A., and others. 2000. *Agricultures familiales et développement rural en Méditerranée.* Paris: Editions Karthala.

Abdrabo, A. 2015. "Conspiracy to Divide Egypt." (In Arabic.) *Al-Shorouk,* February 8. Cairo.

Acemoglu, D., and J. Robinson. 2012. *Why Nations Fail: The Origins of Power, Prosperity, and Poverty.* New York: Crown Publishers.

Al-Sharafat, A., M. Altarawaneh, and E. Altahat. 2012. "Effectiveness of Agricultural Extension Activities." *American Journal of Agricultural and Biological Sciences* 7, no. 2: 194–200.

Amer, Mona. 2012. "The School-to-Work Transition of Jordanian Youth." Working Paper 686. Cairo: Economic Research Forum.

Amin, M., and others. 2012. *After the Spring: Economic Transitions in the Arab World.* Oxford University Press.

Arab Republic of Egypt and Japan International Cooperation Agency. 2002. "Cairo Regional Area Transportation Study (CREATS)." Cairo.

Ardic, O., N. Mylenko, and V. Saltane. 2011. "Small and Medium Enterprises: A Cross-Country Analysis with a New Data Set." Policy Research Working Paper 5538. Washington: World Bank.

Assaad, R., R. Hendy, and C. Yassine. 2012. "Gender and the Jordanian Labor Market." Working Paper 701. Cairo: Economic Research Forum.

Assaad, R., and G. Barsoum. 2007. "Youth Exclusion in Egypt: In Search of Second Chances." Middle East Youth Initiative Working Paper. Washington: Wolfensohn Center for Development, Brookings.

Autor, D., H. Levy, and R. Murnane. 2003. "The Skill Content of Recent Technological Change: An Empirical Exploration." *Quarterly Journal of Economics* 118, no. 4: 1279–1333.

Banerjee, A., and E. Duflo. 2008. "What Is Middle Class about the Middle Class around the World?" *Journal of Economic Perspectives* 22, no. 2: 3–28.

Bayat, A. 1998. "Revolution without Movement, Movement without Revolution: Comparing Islamic Activism in Iran and Egypt." *Studies in Society and History* 40, no. 1: 136–69.

Berrah, K., and M. Boukriff. 2013. "La problématique de la création des entreprises: une application sur les PME Algérienne." Paper presented at the International Conference on Economics and Management of Networks. Université Ibn Zohr, Agadir, Morocco, November 21–23, 2013.

Boughzala, M. 2013. "Youth Employment and Economic Transition in Tunisia." Working Paper 56. Global Economy and Development, Brookings.

Bradley, J. 2012. *After the Arab Spring: How Islamists Hijacked the Middle East Revolts.* New York: Palgrave Macmillan.

Brixi, H., E. Lust, and M. Woolcock. 2015. "Trust, Voice, and Incentives: Learning from Local Success Stories in Service Delivery in the Middle East and North Africa." Washington: World Bank.

Calderon, C., and A. Chong. 2000. "Causality and Feedback between Institutional Measures and Economic Growth." *Economics and Politics* 12, no. 1: 69–81.

Chauffour, J. 2013. *From Political to Economic Awakening in the Arab World: The Path of Economic Integration.* Washington: World Bank.

Comolet, E. 2014. "Jordan: The Geopolitical Service Provider." Working Paper 70. Global Economy and Development, Brookings.

Devarajan, S., and L. Mottaghi. 2015. "MENA Economic Monitor: Towards a New Social Contract; Middle East and North Africa (MENA) Economic Monitor." Washington: World Bank.

Easterly, W., and R. Levine. 2002. "Tropics, Germs, and Crops: How Endowments Affect Economic Development." Working Paper 9106. Cambridge, Mass.: National Bureau of Economic Research.

Education for All Fast-Track Initiative Secretariat. 2011. *Education for All: Fast Track Initiative Promoting Results in Education.* Annual report. Washington.

El-Mahdi, A. 2012. "Improving Opportunities of the Micro and Small Enterprises in Egypt." Brookings.

El-Sissi, A. 2006. "Democracy in the Middle East." United States Army War College Strategy Research Project. Mimeo.

Elbadawi, I., and S. Makdisi. 2011. *Democracy in the Arab World: Explaining the Deficit.* Abingdon, U.K.: Routledge.

Food and Agriculture Organization of the United Nations. 2011. *The State of Food and Agriculture: Women in Agriculture, Closing the Gender Gap.* Rome.

Ghanem, H. 2013. "The Role of Micro and Small Enterprises in Egypt's Economic Transition." Working Paper 53. Global Economy and Development, Brookings.

———. 2014a. "Egypt's Difficult Transition: Why the International Community Must Stay Economically Engaged." Working Paper 66. Global Economy and Development, Brookings.

———. 2014b. *Improving Rural and Regional Development for Inclusive Growth in Egypt.* Working Paper 67. Global Economy and Development, Brookings.

Ghanem, H., and S. Shaikh. 2013. "On the Brink: Preventing Economic Collapse and Promoting Inclusive Growth in Egypt and Tunisia." Project on U.S. Relations with the Islamic World, Brookings.

Gharbi, S. 2011. "Les PME/PMI en Algérie: Etat des Lieux." *Cahier du Lab.RII 238*. Université du Littoral Côte d'Opale.

Gold, Z. 2014. "Egypt's War on Terrorism." *Sada*, May 22. Carnegie Endowment for International Peace.

Grand, S. 2014. *Understanding Tahrir Square: What Transitions Elsewhere Teach Us about the Prospects for Arab Democracy.* Brookings.

Handoussa, H. 2010. "Situation Analysis: Key Development Challenges Facing Egypt." New York: United Nations Development Program.

International Labor Organization (ILO). 2010. *World of Work Report 2010: From One Crisis to the Next?* Geneva.

———. 2011. *World of Work Report 2011: Making Markets Work for Jobs.* Geneva.

Jackle, A., and C. Li. 2006. "Firm Dynamics and Institutional Participation: A Case Study of the Informality of Micro Enterprises in Peru." *Economic Development and Cultural Change* 54, no. 4: 557–78.

Kaufmann, D., A. Kraay, and M. Mastruzi. 2008. "Governance Matters VII: Aggregate and Individual Governance Indicators, 1996–2007." Policy Research Working Paper 4654. Washington: World Bank.

Keefer, P. 2004. "A Review of the Political Economy of Governance from Property Rights to Voice." Policy Research Working Paper 3315. Washington: World Bank.

Kharas, H. 2010. "The Emerging Middle Class in Developing Countries." Working Paper 285. Paris: OECD Development Center.

Kharas, H., and E. Abdou. 2012. "Regulatory Reforms Necessary for an Inclusive Growth Model in Egypt." *Global Views* 37 (November). Brookings (www.brookings.edu/~/media/research/files/papers/2012/11/inclusive-growth-egypt-kharas/11-inclusive-growth-egypt-kharas.pdf).

Levy, F., and R. Murnane. 2004. *The New Division of Labor: How Computers Are Creating the Next Job Market.* Princeton University Press.

Mandri-Perrott, C. 2010. "Private Sector Participation in Light Rail–Light Metro Transit Initiatives." Washington: World Bank.

Matsunaga, H., and M. Ragheb. 2015. "How to Fill the Implementation Gap for Inclusive Growth: Case Study of the Urban Transport Sector in Egypt." Working Paper 85. Global Economy and Development, Brookings.

Ministry of Agriculture and Land Reclamation 2009. "Strategy for Sustainable Agricultural Development 2030." Cairo.

Morikawa, Y. 2015a. "Female Labor Participation in Morocco." Mimeo. Brookings.

———. 2015b. *The Opportunities and Challenges of Female Labor Force Participation in Morocco.* Working Paper 86. Global Economy and Development, Brookings.

Muasher, M. 2014. *The Second Arab Awakening and the Battle for Pluralism.* Yale University Press.

Offenhauer, P. 2005. "Women in Islamic Societies: A Selected Review of Social Scientific Literature." Washington: Library of Congress.

Owen, R. 2012. *The Rise and Fall of Arab Presidents for Life.* Harvard University Press.

Ozar, S., G. Ozartan, and Z. Irfanoglu. 2008. "Micro and Small Enterprise Growth in Turkey: Under the Shadow of Financial Crisis." *Developing Economies* 46 (December): 331–62.

Peattie, Lisa. 1987. "An Idea in Good Currency and How It Grew: The Informal Sector." *World Development* 15 (July): 851–60.

Pritchett, L. 1997. "Divergence, Big Time." *Journal of Economic Perspectives* 11, no. 3: 3–17.

Program for International Student Assessment (PISA). 2009. Paris: OECD.

Qutb, S. 1990. *Milestones.* Translated by Ahmad Zaki Hammad. Indianapolis, Ind.: American Trust Publishers.

Rutherford, B. 2008. *Egypt after Mubarak: Liberalism, Islam, and Democracy in the Arab World.* Princeton University Press.

Sakamoto, K. 2013. "Efforts to Introduce Inclusive Planning in Egypt." Working Paper 54. Global Economy and Development, Brookings.

Samitowska, W. 2011. "Barriers to the Development of Entrepreneurship Demonstrated by Micro, Small and Medium Enterprises in Poland." *Economics and Sociology* 4, no. 2.

Shoeb, Saeed. 2006. "Interview with the General Guide of the Muslim Brotherhood." *Rosa al Yusuf.* April 9 (in Arabic).

Silatech Index Brief. July 2013 (www.silatech.com).

Steer, L., H. Ghanem, and M. Jalbout. 2014. *Arab Youth: Missing Educational Foundations for a Productive Life.* Center for Universal Education, Brookings.

Stone, A., and L. Badawy. 2011. "SME Innovators and Gazelles in MENA: Educate, Train, Certify, Compete." MENA Knowledge and Learning Quick Notes Series. Washington: World Bank.

Tanaka, S., and M. Yoshikawa. 2013. "Establishing Good Governance in Fragile States through Reconstruction Projects: Lessons from Iraq." Working Paper 52. Global Economy and Development, Brookings.

Trends in International Mathematics and Science Study (TIMMS). 2011. International Association for the Evaluation of Educational Achievement (IEA).

United Nations. 2001. "Malaysian Experiences of Monitoring in Development Planning: Development Planning in a Market Economy." Least Developed Countries Series 6. New York.

United Nations Development Program. 2002. "Arab Human Development Report." New York: United Nations.

Wendell, C. 1978. *Five Tracts of Hasan al-Bana (1906–1949).* University of California Press.

Wickham, C. 2013. *The Muslim Brotherhood: Evolution of an Islamist Movement.* Princeton University Press.

Willis, M. 2014. *Politics and Power in the Maghreb: Algeria, Tunisia, and Morocco from Independence to the Arab Spring.* Oxford University Press.

Wittes, T. 2008. *Freedom's Unsteady March: America's Role in Building Arab Democracy.* Brookings.

World Bank. 2003. "Better Governance for Development in the Middle East and North Africa: Enhancing Inclusiveness and Accountability." Washington.

———. 2008. "The Road Not Traveled: Education Reform in the Middle East and North Africa." Washington.

———. 2012a. "Reclaiming Their Voice: New Perspectives from Young Women and Men in Upper Egypt." Washington.

———. 2012b. *Reshaping Egypt's Economic Geography: Domestic Integration as a Development Platform.* Report 71249. Washington.

———. 2013a. "Opening Doors: Gender Equality and Development in the Middle East and North Africa." Washington.

———. 2013b. Project Appraisal Document on a Proposed Grant from the MENA Transitional Fund in the Amount of U.S. $4 Million to the Kingdom of Morocco for the New Governance Framework Implementation Support Project. Washington.

———. 2014a. "Cairo Traffic Congestion Study." Washington.

———. 2014b. "Doing Business 2014: Smarter Regulations for Small and Medium Sized Enterprises." Washington.

———. 2015. *Jobs or Privileges: Releasing Prosperity in the Middle East and North Africa.* Washington.

World Bank, Food and Agriculture Organization of the United Nations (FAO), and International Fund for Agricultural Development. 2009. "Improving Food Security in Arab Countries." Washington: World Bank.

World Bank and Organization for Economic Cooperation and Development (OECD). 2013. *Integrating Human Rights into Development: Donor Approaches, Experiences, and Challenges.* Washington: World Bank.

Index